The question of genocide in Australia's history

AN INDELIBLE STAIN?

HENRY REYNOLDS

VIKING

Viking
Penguin Books Australia Ltd
487 Maroondah Highway, PO Box 257
Ringwood, Victoria 3134, Australia
Penguin Books Ltd
Harmondsworth, Middlesex, England
Penguin Putnam Inc.
375 Hudson Street, New York, New York 10014, USA
Penguin Books Canada Limited
10 Alcorn Avenue, Toronto, Ontario, Canada M4V 3B2
Penguin Books (N.Z.) Ltd
Cnr Rosedale and Airborne Roads, Albany, Auckland, New Zealand
Penguin Books (South Africa) (Pty) Ltd
5 Watkins Street, Denver Ext. 4, 2094, South Africa
Penguin Books India (P) Ltd
11, Community Centre, Panchsheel Park, New Delhi 110 017, India

First published by Penguin Books Australia Ltd 2001

10 9 8 7 6 5 4 3 2 1

Cover design by Cathy Larsen, Penguin Design Studio
Text design by Lynn Twelftree, Penguin Design Studio
Front cover photograph *Children at Barrow Creek, probably 1901–2* from Baldwin Spencer Photographic
Collection, reproduced courtesy of Museum Victoria
Typeset in Perpetua 12.5/15pt by Midland Typesetters, Maryborough, Victoria
Made and printed in Australia by Australian Print Group, Maryborough, Victoria

National Library of Australia
Cataloguing-in-Publication data:

Reynolds, Henry, 1938– .
    An indelible stain? : the question of genocide in Australia's history.

    Bibliography.
    Includes index.
    ISBN 0 670 91220 4.

    1. Genocide. 2. Aborigines, Australian – Treatment. 3. Aborigines, Australian – History.
    4. Australia – Race relations – History. I. Title.

994.0049915

www.penguin.com.au

CONTENTS

ACKNOWLEDGEMENTS

This book was written while I was a recipient of an Australian Research Council Senior Research Fellowship. Colleagues at the Launceston campus of the University of Tasmania made me welcome and allowed me to pursue my writing and research with a minimum of disruption.

I have received assistance in many libraries and archives, but would particularly like to mention the Interlibrary Loans Officer at the University of Tasmania, Launceston campus; Bill Tully at the Australian National Library; and the librarians at the United Nations in New York. I would also like to thank my typist, Jean Willoughby; my agents, Arms and Matthews; and my friends at Penguin Books, particularly Clare Forster, Katie Purvis, Clare Collins and Bob Sessions.

I have benefited by reading the work of those who preceded me along the controversial track of Australian genocide studies, including Tony Barta, Paul Bartrop, Dick Kimber, Dirk Moses, Colin Tatz and Pamela Watson.

I have discussed the subject over the years with numerous people, among whom I would like to note Alison Palmer, who first stimulated my interest in genocide studies; Russell McGregor, with whom I worked closely on the ideas that gave rise to the dying race syndrome; Marilyn Lake, who, with inimitable scepticism, discouraged recourse to easy answers; and Rex Hesline, who generously shared his unrivalled knowledge of early Sydney.

My family – Margaret, John, Anna and Rebecca – have been, as ever, supportive and have frequently re-enforced my commitment to progress along the often difficult road of human rights advocacy. Margaret introduced me to the United Nations in New York and inducted me into its ethos and ideals.

INTRODUCTION

WHILE WRITING THIS text I was more secretive than usual about what I was doing.

When people asked whether I was working on a new book, I was noncommittal and reticent and tried to deflect further inquiries. If possible I avoided the word genocide — it didn't seem to be a subject suitable for brief, casual conversations. And how could my interlocutors respond? By saying, 'How interesting'? By commenting, with irony, on how challenging it must be? Part of my difficulty in discussing the project was that genocide is not a simple matter and there are no easy or clear-cut answers to the question of whether genocide has been committed in Australia.

When I was invited to speak at a recent literary festival breakfast, I was unsure as to what I might talk about. Tradition suggested I should discuss my work-in-progress. But would this book do, I wondered? Could I deal with genocide over muffins? Was smallpox a suitable subject to discuss as we drank our coffee? I had no desire to talk about previous books, having done so many times before and lacking the sense of engagement one has with a work in the process of formation.

Genocide is a confronting subject. It is something that most people have heard of and often hold strong views about. They usually associate it with the mass killing of the Holocaust or perhaps such recent and comparable events in Cambodia and Rwanda. It is not often appreciated that, as defined in the United Nations Genocide Convention, there is much more to the concept than mass murder — that the attempt to destroy a human group in whole or in part can take many forms, not all of them violent.

There is, as well, a more specifically Australian context to the discussion about genocide. On the one hand, there are people who are profoundly disturbed by and often very angry at the suggestion that genocide has ever characterised the relations between Aborigines and settlers. On the other, there are those who feel that there is no other word strong enough to condemn aspects of Australian colonisation — that it is a term of global significance that puts the fate of the Aborigines in its true context.

More specifically, there is the ongoing debate about what has been called the black-armband version of history: the belief of some Australians that a whole generation of scholars has deliberately concentrated — and exaggerated — the less attractive features of our past with an obvious contemporary political agenda motivating their malice. The prime minister, Mr John Howard, appears to share this view and recently declared that the success of the Sydney Olympic Games delivered a huge serve to the nation's detractors, those who portray a negative view of our history.[1] More recently still, he asserted that it was time the community stopped navel-gazing and got on with the future. It was time we 'stopped using outrageous words like genocide'.[2]

So why, in such a contentious climate, would I write a book about genocide? It would seem destined to be tossed on a sea of controversy, likely to be battered from all sides — by those who are hostile to the mere suggestion that such an 'outrageous word' could be applied to Australia and by their opponents, who feel that no other term is powerful enough to capture their anger.

So stormy is the debate that neither side appears to welcome a careful and reasonably dispassionate investigation of the topic. The genocide promoters take the view that to analyse and explain the attitudes and actions of the colonists is, by the very nature of the exercise, to excuse and exculpate. They believe that the colonists' behaviour warrants condemnation, not explanation. For their part, the genocide deniers find the process of examination an unacceptable concession to the view that there might, after all, be something to investigate.

But the question will not go away. It is too important to leave alone in the hope that contemporary passions may cool sometime in the future. I have written this book with the understanding that many readers will disagree with my interpretation of Australian history. Others will argue about the meaning, the adequacy or even the relevance of the Genocide Convention. Many people will seek more definite answers, firmer conclusions and sharper, more clear-cut judgements than I have been able to offer.

One of the constant criticisms of contemporary historians is that they apply their own ethical standards and political views to people and events in the past, making inappropriate and retrospective moral judgements. This is said quite often about genocide, given that the word itself was only coined in 1944 and referred most immediately to the Holocaust. What point is there, it is often asked, in applying such a concept to historical events before the Second World War?

The answer is simple. The man who invented the word genocide and helped draft the Convention, Raphael Lemkin, believed that while the term was new, the phenomenon was as old as history itself. He also thought that among many genocides in the past was the action of the Tasmanian colonial government in the 1820s and 1830s. Numerous international scholars have subsequently supported both these views, as I will show in Chapter Two.

The Australian settlers and their descendants obviously did not use the term genocide — or at least not until the 1950s — but they frequently spoke of 'extermination', 'extirpation' and 'extinction', in many different contexts. These words were in common usage in all parts of Australia — far more so than most readers will have thought possible.

The prospect of extinction was raised in official correspondence between the Colonial Office in London and their governors in Australia. On 5 November 1830 the Secretary of State for the Colonies, Sir George Murray, wrote to Tasmania's Lieutenant-Governor, George Arthur, on the subject of conflict between the settlers and the colony's tribes. Among other things, he referred to the 'great decrease which has of late years taken place in the amount of the Aboriginal population' that suggested it was not unreasonable to apprehend 'that the whole race of these people, may at no distant period become extinct'.

Murray observed:

> But with whatever feelings such an event may be looked forward to by those of the settlers who have been sufferers by the collisions which have taken place, it is impossible not to contemplate such a result of our occupation of the island as one very difficult to be reconciled with feelings of humanity, or even with principles of justice and sound policy; and the adoption of any line of conduct, having for its avowed, or for its secret object, the extinction of the Native race, could not fail to leave an indelible stain upon the character of the British Government.[3]

The question that Murray's words still confronts us with is whether our history has left an indelible stain upon the character and reputation of Australian governments — colonial, State and federal — and upon the colonists themselves and their Australian-born descendants. The following chapters attempt to answer this question.

ONE

Two Canberra cameos

IN JUNE 1949 the Australian parliament debated the Genocide Convention Bill. The bill was designed to approve Australia's ratification of the Convention on the Prevention and Punishment of the Crime of Genocide, which had been adopted by the General Assembly of the United Nations meeting in Paris on 9 December 1948.

Australia had been a keen supporter of the Convention. In his role as president of the General Assembly, Dr H. V. Evatt had facilitated the progress of the draft convention through the UN's fledgling committee system. Australia was among the first countries to sign the document and the nation's delegate in the General Assembly, W. J. Dignam, was vociferous in his condemnation of genocide, arguing that it was 'such a vile act that even savages and wild beasts were incapable of committing it'.[1]

The bill received bipartisan support in the federal parliament, although some opposition members took the opportunity both to attack Dr Evatt and to refer to the contemporaneous Soviet oppression in Eastern Europe. The leader of the opposition, R. G. Menzies, remarked that every member of the parliament would view with equal horror the practice of mass killing and persecution of people to death 'for reasons of race or religion, or for other reasons referred to in the convention'. There would, he declared, be no dispute in the House about the abominable character of the crime of genocide. Persecution of the kind against which the Convention was directed must never be tolerated. Menzies hastened to add that persecution of that sort had 'never been tolerated in Australia'. He concluded his speech by casting doubt on the efficacy of covenants and conventions but declaring in a peroration:

> However the last thing I should dream of doing would be to speak or vote in such a way as to cast any doubt on the proposition that in Australia we abominate the crime of genocide. No-body has ever doubted it. If it needs our subscription to a convention to advertise our feeling to the world, then let us subscribe to it.[2]

In committee, backbenchers added their thoughts to the debate. The member for the Northern Territory, Mr Blain, thought it an insult that the House should be called upon to vote on such a bill because it dealt with a crime 'of which no Anglo-Saxon nation could be guilty'. In fact, he said, the Convention itself was 'an insult to all Anglo-Saxons all over the world' because none of the enumerated crimes 'could ever be committed by the Anglo-Saxon race'.[3] Leslie Haylen, the left-wing Australian Labor Party member for Parkes, made no mention of the Anglo-Saxon race, but his theme was similar to that of his political opponent. He declared:

> That we detest all forms of genocide and desire to remove them arises from the fact that we are a moral people. The fact that we have a clean record allows us to take such an attitude regarding genocide.[4]

The bill then went to the Senate, where it was welcomed by both government and opposition and quickly passed. However, contrary to the widely held expectation at the time that the Australian parliament would move to embody the Convention in domestic legislation, nothing was done until the question of genocide forced its way into the forefront of political life many years later.

So despite some cynicism about the value of international documents and of the United Nations itself, the federal parliament unanimously agreed to Australia's ratification of the Genocide Convention. Many members and senators expressed their abhorrence of genocide in general and of the Holocaust in particular. It seems that no-one thought that the Convention had any direct relevance to Australia. They would undoubtedly have been amazed if they could have known that just under fifty years later their parliamentary successors would be accused of genocide.

On 3 July 1998 four members of the Aboriginal Tent Embassy, the permanent protest set up outside Canberra's Old Parliament House — Wadjularbinna Nulyarimma, Isobel Coe, Billy Craigie and Robbie Thorpe — attended the central Canberra police station and asked the sergeant on duty to issue warrants for the arrest of the prime minister, John Howard, his deputy, Tim Fischer, independent senator Brian Harradine and One Nation leader Pauline Hanson. Howard and Fischer were accused of conspiracy to commit genocide as a result of the federal government's 10-point plan to deal with the consequences of the Wik case, in which the High Court had ruled that native title was not extinguished by pastoral leases. Harradine was accused of complicity in genocide, Hanson with public incitement to commit it.

The sergeant replied that he had never heard of such an offence. Three days later the self-styled Aboriginal Genocide Prosecutors made a request to the registrar of the Australian Capital Territory Magistrates Court to lay charges relating to genocide. The registrar, P. R. Thompson, replied in writing a day later stating that the alleged crimes were unknown to the law of the ACT because the federal parliament had failed to enact legislation which embodied the Genocide Convention in Australian law.

The following day, the four Tent Embassy members delivered letters to every member of the Senate and House of Representatives accusing them of complicity in genocide because of parliament's failure to legislate on the matter, thereby allowing genocide to continue while providing no legal recourse for the victims. They followed this up with formal letters to all 101 foreign embassies and consulates in Australia seeking immediate and urgent assistance to prevent further acts of genocide being committed against the Aboriginal people and, specifically, to gain the support of governments to initiate proceedings against Australia in the International Court of Justice in The Hague.

The case of the Genocide Prosecutors against Australia was outlined in a written submission addressed to the Supreme Court of the ACT on 23 July:

Australia's responsibility for crimes of genocide as defined in the Genocide Convention

The Commonwealth of Australia is responsible for past, present and continuing genocide, conspiracy to commit genocide, direct and public incitement to commit genocide, attempt to commit genocide and complicity in genocide against the original peoples of the land claimed by the Commonwealth of Australia to be under its sovereign jurisdiction.

The original peoples of the land known as Australia occupy all the lands claimed to fall within the territory of Australia.

The Commonwealth of Australia is responsible for:

(a) killing members of each of the original peoples;

(b) causing serious mental and physical harm to members of each of the original peoples;

(c) deliberately inflicting on the original peoples of the land conditions of life likely to bring about the physical destruction of each of the original peoples in whole and in part;

(d) imposing measures intended to prevent births within each of the original peoples;

(e) forcibly transferring children of each of the original peoples to Europeans under the claimed jurisdiction of the Commonwealth of Australia.

The Commonwealth of Australia's responsibility in this matter is made particularly grave by the fact that, had it enacted the necessary genocide legislation in 1949, then the original peoples of the land would have been spared the past 50 years of genocide.

Given that Australia proposed the resolution of the General Assembly (under the then presidency of an eminent Australian) adopting the Genocide Convention on 9 December 1948, and given that the Parliament of Australia in 1949 enthusiastically enacted a statute extending the operation of the Convention to all its territories and promising bi-partisan support for genocide legislation. There is no doubt that in 1949 the Commonwealth of Australia knew precisely and exactly what constituted the crime of genocide and also knew equally clearly how to stop and prevent such crimes by, especially, genocide legislation.

There is also no doubt that the Commonwealth of Australia has known since 1949 that its failure to enact genocide legislation was a grave breach of its international obligations.[5]

The legal issues involved were finally dealt with by the Federal Court of Australia in the case *Nulyarimma v. Thompson* and the judgement was handed down in September 1999. The four Genocide Prosecutors had appealed against an earlier decision of Mr Justice Crispin of the ACT Supreme Court, who had upheld the refusal of the registrar of the Magistrates Court to issue warrants for the arrest of the four politicians. In his leading judgement, the Federal Court's Mr Justice Wilcox observed that while there was much in Australian history that could be construed as genocidal, it was far from clear that the issue at stake – the government's 10-point plan – was in any way related to the intention to destroy the Aboriginal race. The second difficulty for the four appellants was that, lacking appropriate legislation, genocide was not a crime under Australian law.[6]

But the Genocide Prosecutors had done two important things. They had made it clear to the community that genocide was not a crime in Australia; Wadjularbinna Nulyarimma had presented an affidavit to the court which outlined the events of her life, providing a clear picture of the passion and sense of profound injustice that had led to the hope that the prime minister and other leading politicians could be arrested and charged with the crime of genocide.

Wadjularbinna was born into the Gungalidda people of the land adjacent to the Gulf of Carpentaria. She was conceived when her mother was raped by a white man. At the age of three or four she was forcibly taken by the Plymouth Brethren, who ran the Doomadgee Mission. She remembers being snatched out of her grandmother's arms and her grandmother's wailing as she walked away from the mission. She lost contact with her family and never saw her grandmother again. Mission policy was to segregate boys and girls, to raise them in dormitories and keep the children apart from the adults on the mission. Wadjularbinna explained:

> My sister and I could not speak a word of English. We communicated in our own language. We soon learned that we weren't allowed to speak our language, so when we tried to communicate to each other we were dragged off to the bathroom and had our mouths washed out with soap on a face washer. This went on for days, weeks and months until we lost our language completely.[7]

Life in the dormitory was harsh. 'We were treated as slaves', Wadjularbinna recalled, 'because we had to do things military style'. She worked for the missionaries, cooking, carrying water, caring for the children. Punishment was often severe. Senior girls who escaped from the dormitory were chained to trees and flogged with a plaited greenhide leather whip. Some were flogged so hard they 'swelled up and could not move'; others had to be carried away and taken inside to be bathed for days before their health returned.

'This continued trauma and distress', she explained, 'continued through [my] life on that reserve concentration camp'. Her loving parents were near 'and yet so far because [I] could not turn to them'.[8] She thought of herself as just a number in the system, explaining that:

> I realised that each stage of my growing up in that reserve were acts of genocide, not only against me but against members of my family. They were barbaric acts of genocide. It was a deliberate plan to deny me of my true identity and try and destroy my place within a system of law and religion which connects me spiritually to the land, sea and creation.[9]

After marriage with a white grazier, arranged by the missionaries, Wadjularbinna eventually returned to her community. 'I've done a complete circle', she wrote, 'and returned to my clan and the land of my very being only to find my whole People are at the mercy of genocide right up to this very day'.[10]

In response to the ACT Magistrates Court declaration that genocide was not a crime in the ACT – or anywhere else in Australia – Wadjularbinna declared:

> We can ask the question: since the Convention was signed in 1949 why hasn't Australia gone ahead and made laws about Genocide? Is it that they want to continue this Genocide on a People hoping that it will go through and there will come a time when they won't need this Act anyway because we will be all wiped out? That's what it leads me to believe is going on. It is continual Genocide. It hasn't changed. It just takes on different forms and as a victim and survivor of Genocide I have to say: How convenient of Australia not to have to come up with an Act dealing with Genocide.[11]

Wadjularbinna was growing up in the dormitory at Doomadgee when the Genocide Convention was being drafted in the United Nations. She was still there when, in 1949, the Australian parliament ratified it and members agreed that it had no direct relevance to a country that had a clean record in such matters.

What relevance the Genocide Convention has to Australia's history must now be examined. To do so it will be necessary to explore the process which led to the drafting of the Convention, the document itself and the extent to which its provisions have relevance to the history of European–Aboriginal relations.

TWO

THE GENOCIDE CONVENTION
AND ITS INTERPRETATION

THE WORD 'GENOCIDE' was created in 1944 by an émigré Polish jurist, Raphael Lemkin, and was first used in his book *Axis Rule in Occupied Europe*.[1] It was coined, Lemkin explained, to 'denote an old practice in its modern development'[2] and was made from combining the ancient Greek word *genos*, meaning race or tribe, with the Latin *cide*, meaning to kill. Outlining his ideas, Lemkin wrote:

Generally speaking, genocide does not necessarily mean the immediate destruction of a nation, except when accomplished by mass killings of all members of a nation. It is intended rather to signify a co-ordinated plan of different actions aiming at the destruction of essential foundations of the life of national groups themselves. The objectives of such a plan would be disintegration of the political and social institutions, of culture, language, national feelings, religion, and the economic existence of national groups, and the destruction of the personal security, liberty, health, dignity, and even the lives of the individuals belonging to such groups. Genocide is directed against the national group as an entity, and the actions involved are directed against individuals, not in their individual capacity, but as members of the national group . . . Genocide has two phases: one, destruction of the national pattern of the oppressed group; the other, the imposition of the national pattern of the oppressor.[3]

Lemkin's definition of genocide and his advocacy of international action to prevent it in the future grew out of his knowledge of Nazi behaviour during the Second World War, but he did not consider that this was the only example of genocide. He had advocated international action against such crimes at an international legal conference in Madrid in 1933. In a footnote to his chapter on genocide, he provided many examples from the past in which nations and groups of the population were 'completely or almost completely destroyed'. Lemkin's view about the ubiquity of genocide was faithfully reproduced in the preamble to the Convention, which recognised that 'at all periods of history genocide has inflicted great losses on humanity'.[4]

It was the new and shocking knowledge of the Holocaust that fostered the urgent forensic use of Lemkin's new coinage. The word was employed in October 1945 in the indictment of the major German war criminals brought before the Nuremberg Tribunal and was taken up by the fledgling United Nations organisation at its first meeting in December 1946, when it adopted a resolution that read:

Genocide is a denial of the right of existence of entire human groups, as homicide is the denial of the right to live of individual human beings; such denial of the right of existence shocks the conscience of mankind, results in great losses to humanity in the form of cultural and other contributions represented by these human groups, and is contrary to moral law and to the spirit and aims of the United Nations.

Many instances of such crimes of genocide have occurred when racial, religious, political and other groups have been destroyed, entirely or in part.

The punishment of the crime of genocide is a matter of international concern.

The General Assembly, therefore,

Affirms that genocide is a crime under international law which the civilized world condemns, and for the commission of which principals and accomplices – whether private individuals, public officials or statesmen, and whether the crime is committed on religious, racial, political or any other grounds – are punishable;

Invites the Member States to enact the necessary Legislation for the prevention and punishment of this crime;

Recommends that international co-operation be organized between States with a view to facilitating the speedy prevention and punishment of the crime of genocide, and, to this end;

Requests the Economic and Social Council to undertake the necessary studies, with a view to drawing up a draft convention on the crime of genocide to be submitted to the next regular session of the General Assembly.[5]

For the next two years a draft document was written, debated and changed on its way through the United Nations bureaucracy and back to the General Assembly for ratification. The secretary-general, with the assistance of Raphael Lemkin and two other eminent jurists, prepared a draft convention which became the basis for the final document but was significantly changed as it passed before both an ad hoc committee and the Sixth or Legal Committee of the Economic and Social Council. The main provisions of the final draft were:

ARTICLE I

The contracting Parties confirm that genocide, whether committed in time of peace or in time of war, is a crime under international law which they undertake to prevent and to punish.

ARTICLE II

In the present Convention, genocide means any of the following acts committed with intent to destroy, in whole or in part, a national, ethnical, racial or religious group, as such:

(a) Killing members of the group;

(b) Causing serious bodily or mental harm to members of the group;

(c) Deliberately inflicting on the group conditions of life calculated to bring about its physical destruction in whole or in part;

(d) Imposing measures intended to prevent births within the group;

(e) Forcibly transferring children of the group to another group.

ARTICLE III

The following acts shall be punished:

(a) Genocide;

(b) Conspiracy to commit genocide;

(c) Direct and public incitement to commit genocide;

(d) Attempt to commit genocide;

(e) Complicity in genocide.

ARTICLE IV

Persons committing genocide or any of the other acts enumerated in article III shall be punished, whether they are constitutionally responsible rulers, public officials or private individuals.

ARTICLE V

The Contracting Parties undertake to enact, in accordance with their respective Constitutions, the necessary legislation to give effect to the provision of the present Convention and, in particular, to provide effective penalties for persons guilty of genocide or any of the other acts enumerated in article III.

ARTICLE VI

Persons charged with genocide or any of the other acts enumerated in article III shall be tried by a competent tribunal of the State in the territory of which the act was committed, or by such international penal tribunal as may have jurisdiction with respect to those Contracting Parties which shall have accepted its jurisdiction.

ARTICLE VII

Genocide and the other acts enumerated in article III shall not be considered as political crimes for the purpose of extradition.

The Contracting Parties pledge themselves in such cases to grant extradition in accordance with their laws and treaties in force.

ARTICLE VIII

Any Contracting Party may call upon the competent organs of the United Nations to take such action under the Charter of the United Nations as they consider appropriate for the prevention and suppression of acts of genocide or any of the other acts enumerated in article III.[6]

Since 1948 the Convention has been the subject of innumerable studies and much debate. Many of the more controversial issues were discussed during the drafting process by both UN officials and national delegates. These are worth considering, the better to understand the Convention itself and its possible relevance to the history of Australia since 1788.

Perhaps the most contentious question of all arises from the wording of article II, which defines genocide as action 'committed with intent to destroy, in whole or in part, a national, ethnical, racial or religious group'. The absence of provable intent to destroy was a major obstacle in the way of the Genocide Prosecutors in *Nulyarimma v. Thompson* and will continue to frustrate any future litigants trying to secure a conviction for genocide, even when future legislation has embodied the crime in Australian domestic law.

However, the question of intent cannot be avoided. It was central to the discussion that preceded the final drafting of the Convention. It appeared prominently in the draft document prepared by the UN secretary-general. Genocide was there defined as the deliberate destruction of a human group. The secretary-general argued that this literal definition had to be adhered to rigidly, otherwise the idea of genocide would be expanded indefinitely to include many other acts more appropriately dealt with under the law of war, the protection of minorities or respect for human rights. Without a clear and precise definition, two serious difficulties would arise:

> Firstly, there would be a tendency to include under genocide international crimes or abuses which, however reprehensible they may be, do not constitute genocide and cannot be regarded as such by any normal process of reasoning. International law must be built upon a rational and logical basis and exclude confusion and arbitrary opinions; each idea must be properly defined and not overlap others.
>
> Secondly, if the notion of genocide were excessively wide, the success of the convention for the prevention and punishment of what is perhaps the most odious international crime would be jeopardized.[7]

The secretary-general judged that if the definition of genocide were too broad, governments would become suspicious and refuse to ratify the convention. A multiplicity of objectives would lead to a situation where the chief target was missed.

The matter of intent was raised again in the Ad Hoc Committee at its meeting in April 1948 when the French delegate, M. Ordonneau, argued that it was not sufficient to be acquainted with the fact that a group had been destroyed. The reason for that destruction 'had to be determined'.[8] It was generally understood that genocide was motivated by particular malice, or *dolus specialis*, as it was termed.

The matter of intent continued to trouble members of the drafting committee and it was raised specifically in the Sixth or Legal Committee of the General Assembly by the representative of the Soviet Union, who proposed a change of wording replacing 'intent to destroy' with the more objective measure 'aimed at the physical destruction of'. In supporting the amendment, the French delegate put his finger on the fundamental point at issue, arguing that the new wording would 'guard against the possibility that the presence in the definition of the word "intent" might be used as a pretext in the future for pleading not guilty on the absence of intent'. However, the proposed amendment was decisively rejected by a vote of 36 to 11.[9]

The problems created by the inclusion of 'intent' in the Convention have been discussed by many commentators. One of the most influential explained that:

> measures resulting in the partial or total destruction of a group but taken without the intention of such purpose and result do not fall under the definition and therefore do not constitute acts of genocide under the Convention. An act of destruction can be punished as genocide . . . when the intent to destroy the human group involved can be proven regardless of the results of the deed.
>
> When the destruction of a human group, which will be a partial anni-hilation in most cases, has occurred without such intent but merely as a result of an otherwise intended action, there can be no question of genocide as defined in the Convention.[10]

Another related problem is the relationship between genocide and war. In the secretary-general's paper on the draft convention there was a clear distinction between the two. It stated that certain acts that could result in total or partial destruction were in principle excluded from the notion of genocide, namely 'international or civil war, isolated acts of violence not aimed at the destruction of a group of human beings, the policy of compulsory assimilation of a national element, mass displace-ments of population'. In explanation, the secretary-general wrote that:

> War is not normally directed at the destruction of the enemy; such destruction is only the means used by a belligerent to impose his will on the opponent. When that result has been achieved, peace is concluded. However harsh the conditions imposed on the defeated party may be, it retains the right of existence.
>
> The infliction of losses, even heavy losses, on the civilian population in the course of operations of war, does not as a rule constitute genocide.[11]

In a briefing note to the Ad Hoc Committee the UN Secretariat re-emphasised the point, explaining that in the case of foreign or civil war one side may inflict 'extremely heavy losses on the other' but its purpose is to 'impose its will on the other side and not destroy it'. Genocide refers to the actual destruction of a human group, 'not its restriction, ill treatment or oppression'.[12]

Another issue which arose during the drafting process was the question of the extent to which a group must be destroyed before an act committed with that end in mind could be termed genocide. The general view was that genocide related to a large number of the members of a particular group even if the death toll fell far short of its complete exter-mination. In a letter to a United States senate committee, Lemkin argued that the term 'part of a group' was intended to apply to large numbers of people, that the 'destruction in part must be of a substantial nature . . . so as to affect the entirety'.[13]

The question has remained a controversial one. In a submission to a US senate Committee in 1950, the jurist Nehemiah Robinson observed that according to the wording of the Convention the genocidal aim need not be the total destruction of the group,

> but to eliminate portions of the population marked by their racial, reli-gious, national or ethnic features. The definition of a 'group' as an assem-blage of persons regarded as a unit because of their comparative segregation from others would leave open the question whether the aim must be the destruction of the group in the whole of a country, in part of it, in a single town, etc. The addition of the phrase 'in part' undoubtedly indicates that genocide is committed when homicides are done with a connecting aim, i.e., directed against persons with specific characteristics.[14]

An issue that was widely discussed during the drafting process was the question of cultural genocide, which was included in the overall concept at the beginning of deliberations but fell by the wayside as discussion progressed. Lemkin clearly considered it important when he first coined the term 'genocide'. He referred to the destruction of 'the national pattern' of the oppressed group and the imposition of that of the oppressor. He was concerned about the resulting loss of cultural diversity, arguing that:

> The world represents only so much culture and intellectual vigor as are created by its component national groups. Essentially the idea of a nation signifies constructive cooperation and original contributions, based upon genuine traditions, genuine culture, and a well-developed national psychology. The destruction of a nation, therefore, results in the loss of its future contributions to the world.[15]

In his advice to the secretary-general, Lemkin argued that cultural genocide was much more than 'just a policy of forced assimilation by moderate coercion'. It was a policy that by drastic methods 'aimed at the rapid and complete disappearance of the cultural, moral and religious life of a group of human beings'.[16]

The UN General Assembly Resolution 96 of December 1946 echoed these views, asserting that among other things genocide resulted in 'great losses to humanity in the form of cultural and other contributions represented by those groups . . .'[17] The experts who advised the secretary-general disagreed on the desirability of including reference to cultural genocide, but it appeared as article III of the draft convention:

> Destroying the specific characteristics of the group by:
> (a) forced transfer of children to another human group; or
> (b) forced and systematic exile of individuals representing the culture of a group; or
> (c) prohibition of the use of the national language even in private intercourse; or
> (d) systematic destruction of books printed in the national language or of religious works or prohibition of new publications; or

(e) systematic destruction of historical or religious monuments or their diversion to alien uses, destruction or dispersion of documents and objects of historical, artistic or religious value and of objects used in religious worship.[18]

In the secretary-general's commentary on the draft convention the separation of children from their parents was characterised as:

forcing upon the former at an impressionable and receptive age a culture and mentality different from their parents. This process tends to bring about the disappearance of the group as a cultural unit in a relatively short time.[19]

The article relating to cultural genocide was accepted by the Ad Hoc Committee and sent forward to the General Assembly. A motion supporting cultural genocide was decisively rejected, but the action of removing children from one group to another was specifically preserved and incorporated in the final draft of the Convention, emphasising the importance attached to the practice. Discussing the Sixth Committee's adoption of the clause concerning the removal of children, the special rapporteur on the Genocide Convention explained in 1978 that members of the committee had concluded that:

The forced transfer of children could be as effective a means of destroying a human group as that of imposing measures intended to prevent birth or inflicting conditions of life likely to cause death. Since measures to prevent births had been condemned as an act of genocide, there was reason also to condemn measures intended to destroy a new generation.[20]

Once again, intention was all-important. The 'banishment' from the group had to be executed 'with the intent to attack the continued existence of the group as such'. If done for any other reason, the measures may be considered criminal but are not crimes of genocide under international law.[21]

The role of governments was another question debated vigorously during the drafting of the Convention. Discussion in the Ad Hoc Committee in April 1948 covered issues of relevance to the Australian situation. The United States delegate argued that for genocide to be a crime under international law there would have to be governmental participation.

The matter was further refined by other delegates. Mr Askoul from Lebanon referred to a case where a government through weakness or impotence was powerless to prevent one group massacring another. The Venezuelan delegate observed that the United States position did not anticipate the case of a weak government being unable to 'prevent the extermination of a group occupying a distant region'.[22] M. Ordonneau wished to retain the idea of governmental complicity provided that the word was understood in its widest sense. He explained that the 'mere act of granting impunity to a group committing genocide would constitute complicity'.[23]

The twin questions of government involvement and intention are related to several of the acts defined by the Convention as genocidal, including 'Causing serious bodily or mental harm to members of a group' and 'Deliberately inflicting on the group conditions of life calculated to bring about its physical destruction in whole or in part'.

These measures evolved out of two earlier ones in the secretary-general's draft convention, the first of which read:

> Subjection to conditions of life which, by lack of proper housing, clothing, food, hygiene and medical care, or excessive work or physical exertion, are likely to result in the debilitation or death of the individuals.

In the commentary this was referred to as 'slow death'. In such cases, the 'intention of the author of genocide may be less clear' than when massacre or execution is involved. In cases where victims were placed in concentration camps with an annual death rate of 30 to 40 per cent, the intention to commit genocide was unquestionable. But the secretary-general concluded that there were borderline cases where a relatively high death rate could be ascribed to lack of attention, negligence or inhumanity. Though 'highly reprehensible', these would not constitute evidence of intention to commit genocide.[24]

The second related measure in the draft convention was:

> Deprivation of all means of livelihood by confiscation of property, looting, curtailment of work, denial of housing and of supplies otherwise available to the other inhabitants of the territory concerned.

The secretary-general explained that when a government systematically denied to group members the elementary means of survival, it condemned them to a 'wretched existence maintained by illicit or clandestine activities and public charity' and in fact assigned them to death 'at the end of a medium period instead of a quick death in concentration camps'.[25] Once again, the intention of the perpetrator was the critical test. Drost explained that if the actions of authorities were

> not aimed at the group's destruction the measures against the members do not constitute acts of genocide although, of course, they may well amount to common crimes under national law.[26]

Debate stimulated by the drafting process of the Convention did not come to an end once ratification had been achieved. Many of the contentious issues continued to attract attention from diplomats, jurists and other scholars. But however far-ranging, the discussion remained tethered to the actual wording of the document. From a legal point of view, genocide remained what the Convention had declared it to be. The word itself has a quite specific meaning, no matter how broadly some commentators would wish to construe it. It was, after all, coined only four years before the Convention gave it definitive jural meaning. What is more, the man who minted it, Raphael Lemkin, was intimately involved in the drafting process in an endeavour to match the concept with the Convention.

The debate about genocide has been both ubiquitous and continuous. There is a vast scholarly literature on the subject, concerning the application of the Convention and its principles to both contemporary and historic events. Some commentators have sought to keep the definition of genocide sharp and clear, thereby restricting the number of cases that can be considered to have been genocidal. Others are for broadening the definition in order to gather up many more examples from both the past and the present and add them to an expanded casebook of genocide.

Various writers have tried their hand at crafting new definitions of the crime to augment or improve upon the Convention. In 1974 Vahakn Dadrian made one of the first attempts, when he declared that genocide was

> the successful attempt by a dominant group, vested with formal authority and with preponderant access to the overall resources of power, to reduce by coercion or lethal violence the number of a minority group whose ultimate extermination is held desirable and useful and whose respective vulnerability is a major factor contributing to the decision to genocide.[27]

In 1987 John Thompson and Gail Quets put forward a definition that jettisoned the requirement of intent. Genocide, they declared, was

> the extent of destruction of a social collectivity by whatever agents, with whatever intentions, by purposive actions which fall outside the recognized conventions of legitimate warfare.[28]

In 1990 the leading holocaust scholars Frank Chalk and Kurt Jonassohn proposed an alternative definition. Genocide, they argued, was a form of one-sided killing in which a government or other state authority intended to destroy a group with both the group and its membership defined by the perpetrators.[29] Yet another delineation was offered by Helen Fein, who argued that:

> Genocide is sustained purposeful action by a perpetrator to physically destroy a collectivity directly or indirectly, through interdiction of the biological and social reproduction of group members, sustained regardless of the surrender or lack of threat offered by the victim.[30]

Most of those who craft alternative definitions seek in one way or another to widen the terms of the Convention — to include other recognisable groups along with racial, ethnical, religious and national ones; to circumvent the emphasis on intent; and to broaden the means by which genocide could be perpetrated.

Among the many historical and contemporary circumstances that scholars have sought to bring within the compass of their various definitions is the situation of indigenous people in the so-called colonies of settlement, including the United States, Canada, Argentina, Chile, New Zealand, Australia and South Africa. Considerable debate has arisen over whether there is a variant of genocide — colonial genocide — that is pertinent to the historical circumstances of these societies.

There are clearly common themes that run through the histories in question. These indigenous people all experienced dramatic loss of life during the first generation of contact with European settlers, from many causes — introduced diseases, armed conflict, loss of land and the resulting deprivation. The stories are notorious and well known. But was it genocide? Scholars provide varying and conflicting answers to this question. The range is considerable, with some writers arguing that it was genocide without doubt and others rejecting the proposition entirely. Those who stand in between the two camps consider that while some aspects of the colonising process were genocidal, others clearly were not. In her book *Genocide: A Sociological Perspective*, Fein attempted to provide a sharper analysis of the problem, observing that:

Demographic studies seldom disentangle the relative importance and inter-
action of the causes of such decline: 1) diseases imported by settlers to
which the local population lacked immunity; 2) land usurpation and
destruction of the indigenous economy; 3) deculturation and demoral-
ization of the indigenes and alcoholism; 4) wars; and 5) slaughter by the
colonists. Today we are apt to label the second and third causes as ethnocide
and the fifth as genocide. But some would construe genocide more widely
and others more narrowly in these cases.[31]

The question of intent is never far away in discussions of genocide.
Was the killing of indigenous people done with the specific intention of
destroying particular groups, or did it happen as a consequence of action
that had other motives, such as the taking of land, the imposing of a new
order or the pacification of a violent frontier?

A further complication arises in relation to the role of governments
and what responsibility they can be thought to have had for the actions
of frontier settlers often far from the centres of law and administration.
The prominent genocide scholar Israel Charny addressed this question
and sought to define the crime when it occurred in the course of colonisation or consolidation of power:

> It was a case of genocide that was undertaken or even allowed in the course
> of or incidental to the purposes of achieving a goal of colonization or devel-
> opment of a territory belonging to an indigenous people.[32]

In their book *The History and Sociology of Genocide*, Chalk and Jonassohn refer to the situation where European settlers embarked on
campaigns to destroy the indigenous landowners. 'Such devastations',
they observed,

> were often opposed by governments, but their feeble efforts to protect the
> natives were overwhelmed by the settlers' persistent attempts to annihilate
> their Aboriginal neighbours.

These circumstances could not perhaps be defined in a comprehensive way as genocide, say Chalk and Jonassohn, but the many incidents resulting in indigenous death were cases of 'genocidal massacres'.[33]

But could governments be guilty of genocide when they failed to act to stop the killing of indigenous people, cases where 'unintended genocidal consequences are noted' and then are continued or increased?[34] This is a question addressed by R. W. Smith in an essay called 'Human destructiveness and politics', published in 1987. Smith argues that while genocide was usually considered to be a result of premeditated action against a target group, there were situations, as in the colonies of settlement, where the rapid death of the indigenous people produced genocidal consequences that were not originally intended. He observes that this was

> most often the case in the early phases of colonial domination, where through violence, disease and relentless pressure indigenous peoples [were] pushed towards extinction.

For Smith, the crucial question is what was done when the rapid decline of indigenous populations became apparent. With the recognition of the consequences of colonisation the issue changes, for to persist in these circumstances is to 'intend the death of a people'. The distinction, then, between premeditated and unpremeditated genocide is not decisive, 'for sooner or later the *genocidal* is transformed into *genocide*'.[35]

Although Australian history is often referred to by international scholars when discussing colonial genocide (notwithstanding their all too often inadequate knowledge of the subject), there has been little consideration of the matter by local commentators. The major exception is Tony Barta, who has published important articles both here and abroad. In an essay called 'After the Holocaust: consciousness of genocide in Australia',[36] published in 1984, he asks why Australian historians have so warily skirted the question of genocide when the basic fact of our past is the appropriation of the continent 'by an invading people and the dispossession, with ruthless destructiveness, of another'.[37] He argues that the terrible and well-known story of the Holocaust makes it difficult to discuss the general question of genocide, which for most people means only one thing: the murder of six million Jews. As a result, Australians have never seriously been confronted by the idea 'that the society in which they live is founded on genocide'.[38]

Barta realises that he faces the problem of dealing with the absence of clearly expressed intention to eradicate the Aborigines. In fact, official statements of policy towards native people were 'apt to be concerned and protective' while the intentions of most settlers, as individuals, were 'more often than not – at least until they felt threatened – sincerely benign'. However, the very presence and everyday activities of the settlers 'had an effect which was genocidal'. Barta thinks that Australians have to face the fact that historically there is a 'relationship of genocide with the Aborigines which cannot be understood only in terms of a clear intention to wipe them out'.[39]

In a later essay, in an international book on genocide, Barta returns to what he sees as the need for a new interpretation of the concept, which would embrace 'relations of destruction' and remove the emphasis on intention and policy.[40] In summing up his argument he writes:

In Australia very few people are conscious of having any relationship at all with Aborigines. My thesis is that all white people in Australia do have such a relationship; that in the key relation, the appropriation of the land, it is fundamental to the history of the society in which they live; and that implicitly rather than explicitly, in ways which were inevitable rather than intentional, it is a relationship of genocide.[41]

As provocative and challenging as Barta's thesis was, greater controversy arose from similar comments made elsewhere. In the 1979 High Court case of Coe v. Commonwealth of Australia, Mr Justice Murphy observed that the Aborigines did not give up their land peacefully and that they were killed or forcibly removed from their land 'in what amounted to attempted (and in Tasmania almost complete) genocide'.[42]

Two years later a World Council of Churches delegation examined the circumstances of indigenous Australians and in their published report referred in a matter-of-fact way to the genocidal nature of European–Aboriginal relations.[43] At the end of the 1980s the prominent jurist Hal Wootten considered the question of genocide when submitting a report to the Royal Commission into Aboriginal Deaths in Custody. He argued that in its crudest form the policy of assimilation fell within the 'modern definition of genocide'. The attempt to deal with the so-called Aboriginal problem by the taking-away of children fell within that definition.[44]

Wootten's reference to genocide passed with little public comment. This was not the response that greeted similar but more extensive treatment of the question in the report of the Human Rights Commission inquiry into the separation of Aboriginal and Torres Strait Islander children from their families, entitled *Bringing Them Home* and published in April 1997. The reference to genocide, which took up five pages, attracted far more attention than anything else in the 685-page volume. The authors outlined the main provisions of the Genocide Convention and explained that it applied to the transfer of children from one group to another. They pointed out that even the partial destruction of a group could be genocidal and that if the intention of those removing the children were clear, the case was much easier to establish. In a key passage the authors wrote:

> The Inquiry's process of consultation and research has revealed that the predominant aim of indigenous child removals was the absorption or assimilation of the children into the wider, non-Indigenous, community so that their unique cultural values and ethnic identities would disappear, giving way to models of Western culture . . . Removal of children with this objective in mind is genocidal because it aims to destroy the 'cultural unit' which the Convention is concerned to preserve.[45]

To drive the point home, the report observed that the policies of Australian governments continued to embody genocidal practices until the 1960s or even the 1970s and 1980s, as seen in the continued preference for non-indigenous foster and adoptive parents for Aboriginal children. Given the fact that genocide was arguably an international crime from 11 December 1946 with the passage of the General Assembly resolution on the subject, the activities of Australian governments should be called into question, said the report. The authors concluded that:

> The policy of forcible removal of children from Indigenous Australians to other groups for the purpose of raising them separately from and ignorant of their culture and people could properly be labelled 'genocidal' in breach of binding international law from at least 11 December 1946 . . . The practice continued for almost another quarter of a century.[46]

The question of Australia's racist legacy was pursued with even greater determination by Colin Tatz in his pamphlet *Genocide in Australia*, published in 1999. He argued that in a precise legal sense Australia was guilty of at least three, possibly four, acts of genocide. They were:

> first, the essentially private genocide, the physical killing committed by settlers and rogue police officers in the nineteenth century . . . second, the twentieth-century official state policy and practice of forcibly trans-ferring children from one group to another with the express intention that they *cease being Aboriginal*; third, the twentieth-century attempts to achieve the biological disappearance of those deemed 'half-caste' Aborigines; fourth, a *prima facie* case that Australia's actions to protect Aborigines in fact caused them serious bodily or mental harm.[47]

Of equal importance to Tatz's sociological examination of the question were the contemporaneous comments by members of the judiciary in the hearings brought about by the so-called Genocide Prosecutors. In the ACT Supreme Court, Mr Justice Crispin declared that there was 'ample evidence . . . that acts of genocide were committed during the colonisation of Australia'.[48]

In the subsequent Federal Court case *Nulyarimma v. Thompson*, Mr Justice Wilcox remarked that anyone who considers Australian history since 1788 will readily perceive why some people use the term genocide to describe the conduct of non-indigenes towards the indigenous population. He wrote that it was

> possible to make a case that there has been conduct by non-indigenous people towards Australian indigenes that falls within at least four of the categories of behaviour mentioned in the Convention definition of 'genocide': killing members of the group; causing serious bodily harm or mental harm to members of the group; deliberately inflicting on the group conditions of life calculated to bring about its physical destruction in whole or in part; and forcibly transferring children of the group to another group.[49]

But Wilcox appreciated that the question of intent was all-important when considering behaviour that could be construed as genocidal. 'However, deplorable as our history is', he observed, 'in considering the appropriateness of the term "genocide" it is not possible too long to leave aside the matter of intent.' In general he believed that there was not any 'sustained or official intention to destroy the Aborigines' but rather events produced by the attitudes and actions of many individuals, often in defiance of official instructions. However, he argued that some of the destruction of Aboriginal society 'clearly fell into' the category of genocide. Indeed, a notable example of this was

> the rounding-up of the remaining Tasmanian Aboriginals in the 1830s, and their removal to Flinders Island. There are more localised examples as well. Before that date in Tasmania, and both before and after that date on the Australian mainland, there were shooting parties and poisoning campaigns to 'clear' local holdings of their indigenous populations.[50]

In 1949 Australian parliamentarians believed that the Genocide Convention had no relevance to their own country. Fifty years later senior jurists declared that genocide had been committed in the past. It is important to consider how relevant this view is to the interpretation of the relations between European settlers and Aborigines from the arrival of the First Fleet at Sydney Cove in 1788.

THREE

AN EXTRAORDINARY CALAMITY: THE SMALLPOX EPIDEMIC OF 1789

SMALLPOX BROKE OUT among the Aborigines around Sydney Harbour in April 1789. It was an 'extraordinary calamity', as Marine Captain Watkin Tench observed.[1] His colleague David Collins reported that people whose business called them down to the harbour reported daily that they found the bodies of 'many wretched natives of this country' on the beaches and rocks.[2]

When writing to London early in 1790 Governor Arthur Phillip observed that it was

> not possible to determine the number of natives who were carried off by this fatal disorder. It must be great; and judging from the information of the native now living with us, and who had recovered from the disorder before he was taken, one half of those who inhabit this part of the country died; and as the natives always retired from where the disorder appeared, and which some must have carried with them, it must have spread to a considerable distance, as well inland as along the coast. We have seen the traces of it wherever we have been.[3]

The smallpox spread through much of the Murray–Darling Basin, devastating Aboriginal society wherever it struck.

The only direct observation of the epidemic's impact was in and around Sydney itself. Captain John Hunter arrived back in the struggling colony in early May 1789 from Cape Town. When sailing up the harbour he was much surprised that he did not see a single Aborigine on the shore or any canoes on the water. When he landed he was told of the epidemic. He was subsequently deeply shocked when going around the shores and visiting the caves that once sheltered whole families in bad weather and were now full of 'men, women and children, lying dead'.[4]

How much more shocking it must have seemed to the Aborigines themselves. Collins reported the reactions of Arabanoo, who, having been living with the Europeans, was taken down the harbour to look for his kinsfolk. Those who witnessed 'his expression and agony [could] never forget either':

> He looked anxiously around him in the different caves we visited: not a vestige on the sand was to be found of human foot; the excavations in the rocks were filled with putrid bodies of those who had fallen victims to the disorder; not a living person was any where to be met with. It seemed as if, flying from the contagion, they had left the dead to bury the dead. He lifted up his hands and eyes in silent agony for some time; at last he exclaimed, 'All dead! all dead!' and then hung his head in mournful silence, which he preserved during the remainder of our excursion.[5]

The epidemic may well have been the single most destructive event in the history of relations between Aborigines and the European colonists. In itself that does not make it relevant to the present study. But the source of the infection was uncertain at the time and remains so to this day. One possibility is that the epidemic was deliberately or accidentally let loose by someone in the settlement at Sydney Cove. Not surprisingly, this is a highly contentious proposition. If true, it would clearly fall within the ambit of the Genocide Convention, more specifically article 11 clause (b), causing serious bodily or mental harm to members of the group; and clause (c), deliberately inflicting on the group conditions of life calculated to bring about its physical destruction in whole or in part.

In his account of Sydney's foundation years, Tench wondered how smallpox could 'at once have introduced itself, and have spread so widely' given that the British had assumed from their observations that the disease was unknown in New South Wales. He found the onset of the epidemic inexplicable. After he returned to England he added a note to his journal as he prepared it for publication:

No solution of this difficulty had been given when I left the country, in December, 1791. I can, therefore, only propose queries for the ingenuity of others to exercise itself upon: Is it a disease indigenous to the country? Did the French ships under Monsieur de Peyrouse introduce it? Let it be remembered that they had now been departed more than a year; and we had never heard of its existence on board of them — Had it travelled across the continent from its western shore, where Dampier and other European voyagers had formerly landed? — Was it introduced by Mr Cook? — Did we give birth to it here? No person among us had been afflicted with the disorder since we had quitted the Cape of Good Hope, seventeen months before. It is true, that our surgeons had brought out variolous matter in bottles; but to infer that it was produced from this cause were a supposition so wild as to be unworthy of consideration.[6]

Others have frequently exercised their ingenuity in trying to explain that which Tench found inexplicable. Several of his proposals have not stood the test of time. It seems highly improbable that the virus was introduced by either Cook's ships or those of La Perouse, or by even earlier visitors to the coast of Western Australia. Even if smallpox had been experienced in south-eastern Australia at an earlier period, the unblemished faces and bodies of the oldest of the Aborigines indicated that it had been unknown within living memory. More recent investigators have raised the possibility of transcontinental transmission from the north, as a result of the annual visits of Macassans collecting and processing bêche-de-mer. However, most interest in this epidemiological detective story has centred on the query that Tench was most keen to dismiss – on the so-called variolous matter in bottles included among the medical supplies brought from Britain. What variolous matter was, and why it was brought to Australia, therefore requires some explanation.

Smallpox periodically ravaged Britain and other European countries, and there were a number of serious epidemics in the eighteenth century. But in the early years of the century visitors to Turkey brought back knowledge of inoculation. There, the practice was commonplace, as it was in numerous other Asian countries. The method varied but the principle was relatively simple. Assorted variolous matter – liquid from pustules, scabs in dried and powdered form – was inserted in an incision or drawn up the nostrils in order to induce the disease. Given the extreme infectiousness of the virus the variolation, as it was often called, was usually effective and the patient came down with the disease. It was normally in a milder form and the death rate for induced small-pox was much lower than when the disease was picked up in the usual manner. In fact, the death rate was low enough to make inoculation a risk worth taking in order to acquire the lifelong immunity it bestowed.

By the time the First Fleet sailed for Australia, inoculation was widely practised in Britain and had spread from the cities into the rural areas and from the upper classes to the community at large. A leading scholar in the field has termed the period 1752 to 1798 'the age of inoculation'.[7] Writing of the 1780s, he observed:

> General inoculations were now commonplace in villages and market towns throughout the country: the eminent Dr. John Haygarth of Chester observing in 1785 that 'whole villages in this neighbourhood, and many other parts of Britain, have been inoculated with one consent'.[8]

So widespread was knowledge of the process that it was carried out by laypeople in villages all over Britain. Families and individuals inoculated themselves. However, one of the great problems arising from the popularity of the process was that while the inoculi normally suffered from a mild case of smallpox, they were still infectious and when passed on, the virus resumed its normal virulence. The danger was widely understood. Rural parishes and villages began to regulate and control the process and prosecute practitioners for offences such as 'inoculating Sundry persons' and permitting them afterwards 'to go at large, with Infection upon them'.[9]

And so variolous matter – usually in the form of dried and powdered smallpox scabs – was part of every medical kit in the late eighteenth century and was brought as a matter of course to New South Wales. Given the history of inoculation, many people would have known exactly what it was, how it was administered and what effect it had. It was knowledge that had extended far beyond the medical profession and was commonly understood. In that sense smallpox, its aetiology and amelioration by inoculation were more widely understood than any other disease common at the time. By comparison, the causes of waterborne or vector-transmitted diseases were still shrouded in myth and misconception.

The question of the variolous matter at Sydney Cove was discussed in the first authoritative history of smallpox in Australia, written by Dr J. H. L. Cumpston, the Commonwealth Director of Quarantine, and published in 1914.[10] Cumpston referred back to Tench's attempt to explain the inexplicable and dismissed the possibility that smallpox was endemic or had been introduced by Cook, the First Fleet or the French ships. He believed the epidemic was in some way associated with the arrival of a large number of Europeans and that the variolous matter could not 'be dismissed lightly as a possible source of the epidemic'. But he wisely observed that the question could 'never be settled unless some hitherto undiscovered records come to light'.[11]

The controversy — if not undiscovered records — came to light again in 1982 with the publication of research by Australia's leading economic historian, N. G. Butlin. In an Australian National University working paper on the demography of Aboriginal society between 1788 and 1850,[12] he argues that the question of how blacks were infected with smallpox is an important one that should be addressed. By the 1980s many of Tench's propositions had been cast aside, leaving only infection in some way by the early settlers or transmission from the north. Butlin thought that an Asian source seemed 'highly improbable'. On the other hand, he argues, it was 'extremely likely' that the variolous matter was the source of the epidemic. Having stated his premise, Butlin pushes on deeper into controversial territory. 'Was it used deliberately to infect the aborigines?', he asks rhetorically.[13] He notes that smallpox had been so used against the American Indians in the Seven Years War only twenty-three years before the First Fleet sailed for the south land. He argues that risks to the white settlers were minimal and that

> Smallpox could then have been loosed deliberately as a first and possibly the most important shot in the white campaign to capture black resources . . . Transmission to aborigines by authority is certainly possible; so, too, was it as a grudge act by convicts or military guards of stores; and accidental transfer could have occurred arising out of thefts from stores by either convicts or by blacks themselves.[14]

Butlin followed up his ANU paper a year later with the book *Our Original Aggression: Aboriginal Populations of Southeastern Australia 1788–1850.*[15] He returned to the question of the variolous matter and suggested that logically there were four possible causes of infection: transmission by some authority, deliberately or accidentally by convicts, or unwittingly by Aborigines. These were considered briefly in turn. Aborigines, he thought, may have stolen the jars in order to acquire the glass and accidentally triggered the infection. The same could have happened if soldiers or convicts had stolen the jars and then either accidentally or deliberately allowed the infection to spread. Butlin gave closer consideration to the possibility of official transmission or to the action of disgruntled convicts. He felt that Governor Phillip himself should be excluded although even he might have been 'pressured into action'[16] given the precarious state of the colony in the early months of 1789. For their part, convicts had reason to feel especially hostile towards the Aborigines at this time. In March one convict was killed and another seriously wounded on the outskirts of settlement. A party of their friends went out to avenge the death only to be severely beaten themselves. One was killed and seven wounded, 'most part very severely'.[17] For their efforts they were severely reprimanded by the governor and given 150 lashes each.

They had been doubly punished – beaten by the Aborigines and then flogged by the government – and this may have provided a motive for an attempt to infect the Aborigines. 'It was certainly enough to envenom them', Butlin observed, but he may not have appreciated that the six wounded convicts might have been in a position to gain access to the variolous matter. They were in the hospital for some time recovering from their injuries while all the time knowing they faced a severe flogging when they recovered. As we have already seen, it is most likely that the convicts would have been aware of the whole process of inoculation and the danger it presented for the spread of the disease.

Even if we assume the injured convicts had a motive to infect their enemies and the opportunity to gain access to the variolous matter, this does not go any way towards suggesting how the disease might have been actually transmitted. When summing up his thesis Butlin wrote:

> Obviously one can only speculate about these matters. At the very least, it can perhaps reasonably be said that the whites had control of a virus known to be extremely potent and failed in their responsibility. It is possible and quite likely that they deliberately opened Pandora's Box.[18]

At the end of the book Butlin lists a number of general inferences, one of which was that, although the origins of smallpox were obscure, it was possible 'and, in 1789, likely that infection of the Aborigines was a deliberate exterminating act'.[19] He revisited this proposition in a second ANU paper in 1984 and appeared to edge back from the suggestion that deliberate infection was not only possible but also 'quite likely'. In summing up the case, he wrote:

> I have not, in my book, proposed that it was deliberate. I have simply asked historians to face their history and consider seriously the circumstances in which it might have been deliberate. In including deliberate possibilities (along with accidental ones), I do not necessarily imply deliberate policy. If it occurred deliberately, transmission might have been the work of some embittered or deranged individual.[20]

Butlin's second paper was written in response to the criticism he had called down upon himself, criticism that varied in vehemence and seriousness. In an article in the *Bulletin* entitled 'Aboriginal genocide theory lacks evidence', Tim Duncan observed that

> not every community seems receptive to the idea that its founding father was party to a policy which may have included deliberate mass extermination.
>
> Odder still is that the re-interpretation of Phillip has been canvassed without any evidence, in the absence of which historians traditionally remain quiet. More worrying is that the idea has been launched . . . by Australia's most eminent economic historians . . .[21]

In an article in *Quadrant* in March 1985, Emeritus Professor Charles Wilson took Butlin to task for writing imaginary history, explaining that he was unable to stomach the assumption that the first settlers were guilty of the crime of genocide. He concluded that any reading of the letters, dispatches and diaries of the officers who were at Sydney Cove in 1788 and 1789 would inevitably lead to the conclusion that the accusation of deliberate infection was nothing more than 'grotesque fantasy'.[22]

Perhaps the most substantial critics of Butlin's proposition about the introduction of smallpox were two able scholars, Judith Campbell and Allan Frost. They countered the Butlin thesis in two different ways: casting doubt on the likelihood of deliberate or even accidental infection at Sydney, and suggesting an alternative source of the epidemic.[23] Campbell gave fresh life to the idea that smallpox was introduced on the north coast by the Macassans and transmitted across the continent from north to south. She points out that another and later smallpox epidemic that struck Aboriginal communities in Western Australia and South Australia in the 1860s does seem to have begun on the north coast and to have been carried south and east. She observes that the encounters between tribes on the north coast with infectious islanders among the thousands who visited with the monsoon 'drew Aborigines into the scarred mainstream of human history'.[24]

However, evidence for a northern origin of the second visitation of smallpox in the 1830s is far less convincing and the matter remains in contention.[25] Not surprisingly, given the short duration of the European presence in Australia in 1789, there is even less evidence to establish a Macassan origin for the earliest-known epidemic. That being the case, the argument has to depend on probability, Butlin observing:

> Even granted the possibility that the virus may have been introduced from time to time from the north, only some extreme outside chance could have brought the disease from the north to reach Port Jackson for the first time in the 70 to 80 years before the Fleet and to time the arrival of the virus just fifteen months after the Fleet's anchoring. This combination of events cannot be accepted with any reasonable order of probability.[26]

Both Frost and Campbell raise the question of whether the variolous matter would have remained infectious given that it must have been collected at least two years before the onset of the epidemic and brought all the way from Britain. It is an important point, and there must be considerable doubt that the smallpox virus would have remained 'live' enough to infect the Aborigines. However, we can assume that the First Fleet surgeons were aware of the effect of heat and light on their variolous matter, if only from widespread experience in the profession, working in India, the Caribbean and other parts of the tropical and subtropical world. Protecting the variolous matter from heat and light was hardly a new problem in 1788. It is reasonable to suppose also that the surgeons brought dried and powdered scabs, the most durable of the various common agents of variolation, and that they knew of and took whatever precautions they could against the threat of rapid deterioration.

Frost indicates other difficulties of finding any means of substantiating Butlin's case concerning deliberate or accidental infection. For most of the time when the infection would have to have been transmitted – that is, in the month or so before April 1789 – the Aborigines avoided the Europeans and do not seem to have been in the settlement. How secure the medical supplies were and who might have access to them, legitimately or not, is impossible to say. Frost assumes that, because the governor and the doctors knew that smallpox was a highly dangerous disease, it 'is not realistic to suppose that there was no system of security'.[27] However, this assumes that the doctors thought the variolous matter was still active, which Frost doubts. It also assumes that the security was sufficient to prevent theft of some of the contents of the bottles. He observes that while other thefts were noted in the records, there is no mention of any loss of medical supplies. But the extraction of a small amount of powder, which is all that would have been required, may not have ever been noticed. So, lacking any solid evidence, the most that can be said is that we have no real idea whether variolous matter could have been stolen or not. Perhaps it could have been taken and perhaps it would still have been active enough to infect a person with absolutely no immunity. But that is as far as the argument can progress.

Access would have presented less of a problem if the transmission was 'by some authority', which Butlin thought a logical possibility.[28] There is no evidence at all to support the proposition, as numerous critics pointed out at the time of the controversy in the early 1980s. That is hardly surprising. Putative perpetrators would have been assiduous in hiding their tracks. What we know of the reactions of senior officials — or rather those like Phillip, Collins, Tench, Hunter and Bradley, who left written records — gives little credence to their personal involvement. They seemed genuinely surprised by the outbreak and then reacted with concern and compassion towards the few victims who were brought into the settlement. Frost observed that:

> Given that the colony's officials cared for the sick Aborigines in this humane way, treating them as they would have their own people, it makes no logical sense to suppose that they first deliberately infected them.[29]

It is a cogent argument, but Frost moves on to clinch his case with the assertion that there 'are no grounds whatsoever for supposing they deliberately opened "Pandora's Box"'. But, as Butlin points out, there were many other officials, both military and civil, and we cannot presume to know that each and every one of them would have been incapable of infecting the Aborigines. Actual and presumed use of smallpox in North America should make us wary of any untested presumption of collective innocence.

Butlin referred to the best-known case of the use of smallpox: in 1763 at Fort Pitt in western Pennsylvania during Pontiac's Rebellion. In an infamous incident, two visiting Indian chiefs on a diplomatic mission were given blankets taken from the smallpox hospital. The evidence indicates that the action was both deliberate and calculated. In a recent article, 'Biological warfare in eighteenth-century North America', E. A. Fenn observes that the fort's account books make it clear that British military officers 'both sanctioned and paid for the deed', with knowledge and approval for the action reaching the highest level in the army.[30] General Thomas Gage signed without comment an invoice for two blankets and two handkerchiefs, which specified that they had been 'taken from people in the Hospital to Convey the Smallpox to the Indians'.[31]

Independent of the action at Fort Pitt, the commander-in-chief of British forces, Sir Jeffrey Amherst, wrote to Colonel Henry Bouquet in Philadelphia in July 1763 about the Indians. 'Could it not be contrived to Send the *Smallpox* among those Disaffected tribes?' he asked rhetorically, and then responded by observing: 'We must, on this occasion, use Every Stratagem in our power to Reduce them'. In a second note written a week later, Amherst instructed:

> You will do well to try to Inoculate the Indians by means of Blanketts, as well as to try Every other method that can serve to Extirpate this Execrable Race.[32]

The use of smallpox to destroy the Indians was, then, openly and urgently advocated by the aristocratic Amherst, the most senior military figure in the American colonies. Reflecting on the Fort Pitt situation, Fenn argues that:

> The fact that a single wartime outbreak could prompt two independent plans of contagion suggests that the Fort Pitt incident may not have been an anomaly. Evidence from other fields of battle indicate that in the minds of many, smallpox had an established, if irregular, place in eighteenth-century warfare.

Fenn believes that the Fort Pitt incident was only 'one in a string of episodes' in which military officers in North America 'may have wielded *Variola* against their enemies'.[33] This is an assessment supported by the most recent international study of the history of biological warfare, which concludes that while much evidence is undetailed and uncorroborated in aggregate, it hints at a history of 'sporadic British and American efforts' to infect North American tribes with smallpox 'possibly extending over centuries'.[34]

In developing her argument, Fenn concludes that smallpox was used by the British army against the American forces in the War of

Independence by inoculating individuals who were then sent as refugees into the enemy's camp in the hope of spreading the infection. Given the prevalence of smallpox at the time, it is impossible to determine whether the strategy was in fact adopted and, if so, whether it had the desired effect. Senior American figures, including Washington, Jefferson and Franklin, were convinced that the British were attempting to use smallpox as an offensive weapon.[35] The whole question is, not surprisingly, contentious. At best the evidence is circumstantial and we should treat with caution claims made about enemies in the middle of a war.

Writing about the American siege of Quebec in July 1776, Jefferson explained that he had been informed by officers

> who were on the spot, and whom I believe myself, that this disorder was sent into our army designedly by the commanding officer in Quebec. It answered his purposes effectually.[36]

Washington came to the same conclusion during the American siege of Boston in December 1775. On the 14th of the month he wrote that British troops were 'under inoculation'. It was, he observed, 'a weapon of Defence they are using against us'.[37] In another letter he wrote:

> The information I received that the enemy intended Spreading the Smallpox amongst us, I could not Suppose them Capable of – I now must give Some Credit to it, as it has made its appearance on Severall of those who Last Came out of Boston.[38]

The British commander in Boston was General Gage, who had approved the use of smallpox against the Indians fourteen years before. Two of his junior officers were to have important positions in the First Fleet when it sailed from Britain eleven years later. Major Robert Ross was Lieutenant-Governor and Commander of the Marine; Collins was Deputy Judge-Advocate and Secretary to Governor Phillip.

The North American experience with smallpox does not necessarily have any direct relevance to Australia, but it suggests that British soldiers serving in that theatre would have been aware that smallpox could have a dramatic impact both on the overall strategic situation and on the outcome of particular battles and sieges, as it did dramatically in the failed American siege of Quebec. It is possible that anyone in the army in North America would have heard talk of the use of smallpox as a weapon or been aware of its actual or threatened use against the rebellious colonists.

If the British army did attempt to spread smallpox among their American adversaries and the disease did have an established, if irregular, place in eighteenth-century warfare, it increases the possibility that the epidemic may have been deliberately induced in Australia. It ceases to be a supposition so wild that it can't be considered, but no fresh evidence can be provided to substantiate whatever suspicions may be held. Despite the debate and controversy following the publication of Butlin's work in the early 1980s, we are not much further ahead than we were in 1914, when the Commonwealth Director of Quarantine declared that the surgeons' variolous matter could not be dismissed lightly as a possible source of the epidemic.

However, while the question of smallpox is surrounded with uncertainty, many scholars are convinced that the colonial authorities in Tasmania were guilty of genocide.

FOUR

TASMANIA: A CLEAR CASE OF GENOCIDE?

GENOCIDE OCCUPIED THE attention of the Tasmanian parliament over several days in June 1993. The Liberal premier, Ray Groom, declared that genocide had never taken place in the history of the State.[1] His views were supported by the Hobart *Mercury*, where an editorial asserted that there was 'certainly no policy of deliberate extermination of the Aboriginal people'.[2]

Groom was attacked by the Greens member and spokesperson on Aboriginal affairs, the Rev. Lance Armstrong, for attempting to rewrite history. The premier's statement was the 'most incredibly inaccurate and offensive speech' that Armstrong had ever heard. He countered by saying that while the policy of genocide 'was never openly admitted', the reality was there to be discovered by any reasonable student of history. 'Attempted genocide', he declared,

> was the reality at every step. Aboriginal people were killed; Aboriginal people were dispossessed of their land; Aboriginal people were denied the whole range of human rights . . . The point is that Aboriginal people were massacred and the authorities did nothing about it. Genocide was the policy.[3]

Armstrong had the local historians on his side. In his *History of Tasmania*, published ten years earlier, L. L. Robson argued that the colony's story represented 'an impressive example of extermination'.[4] Australia's leading economic historian, N. G. Butlin, agreed, asserting that after 1825 'genocide directed and organised by the governor substantially eliminated the indigenous population'.[5] Robert Hughes added his powerful voice to the chorus in his bestselling book *The Fatal Shore,* informing readers around the world that what happened in the colony in the 1820s and 1830s was the only true genocide in English colonial history.[6]

The consensus among international genocide scholars is even more marked. Tasmania is usually counted as the site of one of the world's authentic cases of genocide despite the fact that few of the scholars display any first-hand knowledge of Tasmanian history. Indeed, ignorance appears to encourage sweeping and definitive pronouncements. Raphael Lemkin considered Tasmania the site of one of the world's clear cases of genocide,[7] and in one of the first major works on the subject, published in 1981, Leo Kuper referred to the 'systematic annihilation' of Aborigines in Tasmania.[8] In 1986 Ward Churchill, seeking to craft a functional definition of genocide, referred to those cases in which the intention was to destroy the whole population of specific groups, 'such as Tasmania and Cambodia'.[9] The prominent biologist Jared Diamond contributed his opinion in 1985, contrasting those situations where people have died en masse as a result of callous actions not designed specifically to kill them, with well-planned genocides including that of the Tasmanians, the Armenians by the Turks during the First World War, and the Jews by the Nazis during the Second.[10] A similar assessment and comparison was made by Florence Mazian in her 1990 book *Why Genocide?*. The crime, she concluded, was not always as blatantly practised as it was with the Nazis, nor with as much ruthlessness as in the case of the British in Tasmania or the Dutch in South Africa.[11]

In an article in the *New York Review of Books* in 1995, Bernard Bailyn contrasted the Tasmanian experience with the Indian wars of the early United States, declaring that in the British colony the goal of policy was extermination. Three years later, D. C. Watt, Professor of International History at the London School of Economics, contributed his perception of Tasmanian history to the ongoing, informal international colloquium in a review in the *Times Literary Supplement*. The two greatest pre-twentieth-century examples of racial elimination, he declared, were the destruction of the Indians of Patagonia and the 'aboriginal inhabitants of Tasmania'.[12] In a follow-up letter he set out to define what he meant by genocide and in the process referred again to Tasmanian history. He wrote:

> What distinguishes murder from manslaughter and accidental death is the motive of the killer. This is equally true of genocide – in two ways. For an individual German to kill a Jew or a Gypsy, just because of the race of the victim, is an act of genocide. But to accuse the machinery of State under which such killings took place as an act of policy requires proof that this is their aim. There is ample proof that this was the aim of the 'Final Solution'. Jews were to be killed because they were not human, just as the Tasmanian Aborigines were hunted to death for the same reason.[13]

One of the most perverse international assessments of the history of the Tasmanian Aborigines appeared in the major 1990 work *The History and Sociology of Genocide*, edited by distinguished genocide scholars Chalk and Jonassohn.[14] Among a series of case studies from different periods of history and various parts of the world, the editors included an essay by James Morris entitled 'The Final Solution down under', originally published in 1972.[15] Morris tells a conventional tale of the Black Line – the highly organised sweep across the Island by 2200 troops and settlers in 1830 – and the subsequent rapid decline of population on Flinders Island, where the Aborigines 'wasted away, ceased to have babies, and grew thinner and more morose and more helplessly melancholic' because they were 'losing heart'.[16] The most surprising aspect of the piece is its extraordinary characterisation of the Tasmanians. Morris describes them simplistically, sentimentally and patronisingly. Physically, he wrote, the Aborigines seem to have lacked stamina; they were not very strong 'nor very fast, nor even particularly agile, though they were adept at running on all fours'. They looked homely but 'oddly wistful, like elves, or perhaps hobbits'. In fact they seemed an 'insubstantial people'. They lived on the edge of the world and 'seem to have been on the edge of reality too'. Even their language, Morris declared, was rudimentary and was merely 'a series of disconnected words with no linked grammar'. To nearly everything about the Tasmanians there was 'a haunting naivete'; they lived all by themselves 'like children in the woods'.[17]

That such an insubstantial piece should be included in a major international study of the history of genocide is an indication of how little is known about Tasmania by this community of scholars, the members of which almost automatically include Tasmania in their list of genocidal tragedies. In order to advance the discussion it is necessary to have both a theoretical understanding of the subject and a knowledge of the fine detail of Tasmanian colonial history. It is necessary to consider the attitudes of the settlers, the policies of the imperial and colonial governments, the precise nature and purpose of the Black Line, and the institutional history of Wybalenna Settlement on Flinders Island.

During the period of intense frontier conflict between 1826 and 1833, the Tasmanian settlers publicly discussed the matter of genocide. They used the words 'exterminate' or 'extirpate', the latter literally meaning to destroy by uprooting or tearing out. William Barnes, a justice of the peace, landowner and brewer, wrote to Governor Arthur in March 1830 expressing his alarm about continuing Aboriginal hostility. If acts of mutual vengeance did not cease, he remarked, 'then the dreadful alternative only remains of a general extermination by some means or other'.[18]

Rural landowner George Espie informed the official government committee set up to deal with the Aboriginal question that in his view the country must either belong to the Black or the White and that he could see 'no other remedy but their speedy capture or extermination'.[19]

Temple Pearson, another prominent settler, gave similar advice to the colonial secretary in June 1830, arguing that:

> Total extermination, however severe the measure, I much fear will be the only means left to the Government to protect the Whites.[20]

The director of the Van Diemen's Land Company, Edward Curr, added his voice to the brutal clamour, outlining what he saw as the dilemma faced by the government:

> If they [the settlers] do not abandon the Island [and will not] submit to see the white inhabitants murdered one after another . . . they must undertake a war of extermination on principles of which many will be disposed to question . . .

He believed the matter would end, 'as all such matters have ended in other parts of the world, by the extermination of the weaker race', although he shuddered at the idea of 'butchering the poor natives in the mass'; it was 'dreadful to contemplate the necessity of exterminating the aboriginal tribes'.[21]

The colonial newspapers regularly reported on conflict in the interior and at times called for the destruction of the tribes. In 1826, after reporting several murders of frontier shepherds, the editor of the *Colonial Times* declared:

> We make no pompous display of Philanthropy – we say unequivocally, SELF DEFENCE IS THE FIRST LAW OF NATURE – THE GOVERNMENT MUST REMOVE THE NATIVES – IF NOT, THEY WILL BE HUNTED DOWN LIKE WILD BEASTS AND DESTROYED.[22]

In February 1830 the editor of the *Tasmanian* remarked that the Aborigines were displaying a determination to destroy all before them. 'Extermination', he declared, 'seems to be the only remedy'.[23]

The *Independent* reported in September 1831 that following the spearing of a prominent settler, Captain Thomas, several correspondents had written in arguing that 'nothing but a *war of extermination* now remains to be applied'.[24] A fortnight later the editor himself looked forward with foreboding to the return of spring and the prospect of renewed Aboriginal attacks. 'Even their warmest advocates', he wrote,

> must, we fear, admit that unless something forthwith be done by the government, the end will be, horrible as the idea is, EXTERMINATION, as the only means of securing our settlers from their cruel and indiscriminate attacks.[25]

But there were defenders of the Aborigines who, fearing the total destruction of the tribes, called for a radical redirection of policies and attitudes. The surveyor-general, George Frankland, gave a powerful speech at a dinner of the scientific–cultural Van Diemen's Land Society in January 1830 lamenting the fact that, instead of bringing benefits, the colonists had 'heaped ruin and destruction upon those children of misfortune', the owners of the soil, who with better treatment might have been 'rendered valuable friends, and have continued a happy nation'. He hoped there was still time to restore that harmony which had been shattered by the 'brutal inhumanity of white men'. He called on the society to ameliorate the condition of the Aborigines and save them from extirpation.[26]

The involvement of the whole community in the Black Line in 1830 stimulated public debate on the objectives of government policy. The *Colonial Times* reported that in Hobart 'all was ardour and emulation among many of the Whites, trying who should hunt, kill and destroy the most'.[27] Writing to his wife from Launceston, George Augustus Robinson observed that nothing could be heard but talk of 'extirpating the original inhabitants'.[28]

The most interesting public debate on the conduct of the Black Line took place during 'a very general and respectable meeting of the inhabitants' at the courthouse in Hobart late in September 1830. The colony's prominent men addressed, in their different ways, the question of the destruction of Aboriginal society. J. T. Gellibrand, lawyer and former attorney-general, denounced the forthcoming action. 'How dreadful', he declared,

> is it to contemplate that we are about to enter upon a war of extermination, for such I apprehend is the declared object of the present operation and that in its progress we shall be compelled to destroy the innocent with the guilty.[29]

Among the numerous speakers who stood up to oppose Gellibrand, the most articulate – and influential – was Alfred Stephen, the colony's solicitor-general. He told the meeting that he spoke as an individual and not in his official capacity, the newspaper reporting him saying:

> I have before stated, that I act on this occasion in every particular whatever in the capacity of a private individual, without the slightest reference to my character as a Public Officer, and I have to add – the sentiments and opinions which proceed from me are entirely my own, without any connection whatever with those of others, or that there is any wish or opinion entertained which I give utterance to. I beg that this may be distinctly understood – I speak my own individual sentiments without any reference whatever to those held in another quarter. I take this opportunity of noticing Mr Gellibrand's observations as to the taking of the lives of the blacks. I agree with Mr Horne [an earlier speaker] that the slaughter of the whites has been as indiscriminate as any which can be the result of the proposed operation – and I say, that as they have waged such a war upon the settlers, you are bound to put them down. I say that you are bound to do, in reference to the class of individuals who have been involuntarily sent here [the convicts], and compelled to be in the most advanced positions, where they are exposed to the hourly loss of their lives. I say, sir (Mr Stephens here spoke with much animation), that you are bound upon every

principle of justice and humanity, to protect this particular class of individuals, and if you cannot do so without extermination, then I say boldly
and broadly exterminate! I trust I have as much humanity as any man who
hears me, but I declare openly, that if I was engaged in the pursuit of the
blacks, and that I could not capture them, which I would endeavour to do
by every means in my power. I would fire upon them . . . I expose myself,
I am aware, thereby to much attack on the grounds of humanity, but I am
satisfied that we are bound to afford all possible protection to those who
are exposed to the attacks of the blacks, and therefore I am of the opinion –
capture them if you can, but if you cannot, destroy them.[30]

It was a powerful speech, but as Stephen so carefully and precisely
explained, he spoke as an individual and not on behalf of the government.
And indeed, to pursue the question of genocide it is essential to consider
the policies of both the British government, as shaped and implemented
by the Colonial Office, and that of the local administration of Colonel
George Arthur, who governed Tasmania from 1824 to 1836.

The imperial authorities pursued contradictory policies towards the
Aborigines in Tasmania and New South Wales during the first forty years
of settlement. Governors were exhorted to treat the tribes with amity
and kindness while according no recognition to Aboriginal ownership of
land. They counselled peace but sanctioned the use of military force and
declarations of martial law when the Aboriginal tribes resisted the incursions of the settlers and their flocks and herds.

The instructions given to both Governor Arthur and Governor
Darling of New South Wales (1825–31) illustrated the problem. The
governors were encouraged to promote religion and education among
the indigenous subjects, and to

Especially take care to protect them in their persons, and in the full
enjoyment of their possessions, and that you do by all lawful means prevent

and restrain all violence and injustice which may in any manner be practised against them.[31]

But the realities of frontier life and the endemic conflict on the outer
fringes of settlement called forth much harsher instructions concerning
the 'manner in which the Native Inhabitants' were to be treated when
making 'hostile incursions for the purpose of plunder'. Darling and
Arthur were informed by the secretary of state, Lord Bathurst, in 1825:

> you will understand it to be your duty, when such disturbances cannot be
> prevented or allayed by less vigorous measure, to oppose force by force,
> and to repel such Aggressions in the same manner, as if they proceeded
> from the subjects of an accredited State.[32]

Arthur was handed these instructions in person by Darling, who landed
in Hobart in November 1825 on his way from England to New South
Wales. Arthur clearly saw them as an authoritative guide to action and
read them to his officials at critical moments during the campaign against
the Aborigines.

When faced with the rising tempo of violence in Tasmania, the
Colonial Office accepted Arthur's explanations and sanctioned his actions
while continually counselling restraint. Responding in May 1828 to
Arthur's desire to force the Aborigines away from the settled districts,
Secretary of State Huskisson observed that it was difficult to conciliate
and civilise 'these unfortunate beings' while their 'restless Character
would seem to render it extremely difficult to confine them to any
particular limits within the Colony'. But Arthur was urged to proceed
with caution 'in the spirit of utmost kindness' in order to contain
Aboriginal hostility.[33]

Nine months later, when responding to the governor's proclamation declaring that the Aborigines should leave the settled district,
Huskisson's successor, Sir George Murray, was supportive. He indicated
that he appreciated the difficulty of convincing the Aborigines to

'acknowledge any authority short of absolute power', particularly when they were 'possessed with the idea which they appear to entertain in regard to their own rights over the country' in comparison with those of the colonists. But Arthur was cautioned about going too far, Murray writing:

> I cannot, however, omit to impress upon you my earnest desire that no unnecessary harshness may be exercised in order to confine the Coloured Inhabitants within the boundaries you have fixed.[34]

In August 1829 Murray approved, in retrospect, the declaration of martial law the previous November, but it was with 'extreme regret' and the hope that the measure would both 'secure the lives and properties of the settlers and benefit the Natives themselves'.[35]

In November 1830 Murray refused to accept the suggestion made by the official Aborigines Committee that Aboriginal aggression proceeded from a 'wanton and savage spirit inherent in them'. With lofty disdain he observed that in order to accept this opinion it would be necessary to establish that aggressions 'had not begun with the new settlers'.[36] Surveying the troubled relations between settlers and Aborigines, he wrote:

> Although it is greatly to be feared that much time and pains will be requisite to alter the footing upon which the British Settler and the Aborigines of the colony unfortunately stand towards one another, I cannot conclude this Dispatch without urging upon you, in the strongest manner, to continue to use your utmost endeavour to give to the intercourse between them a less hostile character than it now has; and to employ every means which kindness, humanity and justice can suggest, to reclaim the Natives from their original savage life, and render them sensible to the advantages which would ultimately result to themselves, and to their descendants, from the introduction amongst them of the religion and the civilization of those whom it must be difficult for them to regard at present in any other light than as formidable intruders. With this object in view, the utmost

forbearance will be requisite on the part of the settlers, in every case in which a Native may fall in their way, and I hope you will be able by degrees, to prevail upon the settlers to believe that such a line of conduct, both on their own part, and on that of their assigned servants, will not only be the most proper and becoming, but will also prove, in the end, to be the most conducive to their interests and their security.[37]

In June 1831, when the failure of the Black Line became known in London, Viscount Goderich observed that Arthur's strategy had been well calculated to afford security to the colonists for their lives and property 'with the least possible injury to the unhappy beings you were forced to treat as enemies'. He complimented Arthur on his humanity 'towards a race entitled by the wrongs which they have suffered to much forbearance, even while it was necessary to repel their attacks'.[38]

The most compelling and relevant piece of evidence regarding the decline of the Aboriginal population was provided by Sir George Murray in his letter to Arthur in November 1830. He directed his attention to the main question at issue, writing:

The great decrease which has of late years taken place in the amount of the aboriginal Population, renders it not unreasonable to apprehend that the whole race of these people may, at no distant period, become extinct. But with whatever feelings such an event may be looked forward to by those of the Settlers who have been sufferers by the Collisions which have taken place, it is impossible not to contemplate such a result of our occupation of the Island, as one very difficult to be reconciled with feelings of humanity or even with principles of justice and of sound policy: and the adoption of any line of conduct having for its avowed or for its secret object, the extinction of the native race, could not fail to leave an indelible stain upon the character of the British Government.[39]

The question that must now be addressed is this: Did the administration of Governor Arthur adopt policies that had for their avowed or secret object the 'extinction of the native race'? Were its senior members guilty of what we now call genocide?

Arthur arrived in Tasmania in 1824 predisposed to humanitarian policies towards the Aborigines. He was an evangelical Christian, an acquaintance of leading antislavery activists, with a reputation for defending the rights of indigenous people. He had attempted to free enslaved Indians when he was Superintendent of British Honduras between 1814 and 1822, in the face of strong opposition from the local oligarchy.

Arthur's first public statements about the Aborigines were aglow with good intentions. A proclamation was sent to all the magistrates with instructions to give it wide publicity, 'enjoining the utmost attention to the full intent and meaning of it'. It was an important document and deserves to be quoted in full.

Whereas it has been represented to his Honour the Lieutenant-Governor, that several Settlers and others are in the habit of maliciously and wantonly firing at, injuring and destroying the defenceless Natives and Aborigines of this island.

And whereas it is commanded by His Majesty's Government, and strictly enjoined by his Excellency the Governor-in-Chief, that the Natives of the Colony and its dependencies shall be considered under British government and protection.

These instructions render it no less the duty than it is the disposition of his Honour the Lieutenant-Governor to support and encourage all measures which may tend to conciliate and civilize the Natives of the island, and to forbid and prevent, and, when perpetrated, to punish, any ill-treatment towards them.

The Natives of this island being under the protection of the same laws which protect the settlers; every violation of those laws in the persons or property of the natives shall be visited with the same punishment as though committed on the person or property of any settler. His Honour the Lieutenant-Governor therefore declares his determination thus publicly, that if after the promulgation of this proclamation, any person or persons shall be charged with firing at, killing, or committing any act of outrage or aggression on the native people, they shall be prosecuted for the same before the Supreme Court.

All magistrates and peace officers, and other His Majesty's subjects in this colony, are hereby strictly required to observe and enforce the provisions of this proclamation, and to make them known more especially to stock-keepers in their several districts, enjoining them not only to avoid all aggression, but to exercise the utmost forbearance towards the Aborigines, treating them on all occasions with the utmost kindness and compassion.[40]

Unfortunately, benign intentions could not survive the brutal realities of life in the bush as the settlers took up the best land. Aboriginal resistance intensified from the spring of 1826. Having put down a threatening wave of bushranging during 1825 and 1826, Arthur was faced with a far more dangerous guerilla war between settlers and Aborigines, which raged across the so-called settled districts in the river valleys of central Tasmania between Hobart and Launceston. In November 1826 he issued a public statement condemning the series of outrages that had been 'perpetrated by the Aborigines of the colony' and setting out six conditions that could justify settler violence or, as it was phrased, action, 'in the execution of the justifiable measures to which they may have recourse'. They were:

1st. If it should be apparent that there is a determination on the part of one or more of the native tribes to attack, rob, or murder the white inhabitants generally, any person may arm, and, joining themselves to the military, drive them by force to a safe distance, treating them as open enemies.

2d. If they are found actually attempting to commit a felony, they may be resisted by any person in like manner.

3d. Where they appear assembled in unusual numbers, or with unusual arms, or, although neither be unusual, if they evidently indicate such intention of employing force as is calculated to excite fear, for the purpose of doing harm, short of felony, to the persons and property of any one, they may be treated as rioters, and resisted if they persist in their attempt.

4th. If they be found merely assembled for such purpose, the neighbours and soldiers armed may, with a peace officer or magistrate, endeavour to apprehend them; and if resisted, use force.

5th. If any of the Natives have actually committed felonies, the magistrates should make such diligent inquiries as may lead to certainty of the persons of the principals, or any of them (whether this consists in knowledge of their names, or any particular marks or characteristics by which these persons may be distinguished), and issue warrants for the apprehension of such principals. The officer executing a warrant may take to his assistance such persons as he may think necessary; and if the offenders cannot otherwise be taken, the officer and his assistants will be justified in resorting to force, both against the principals and any others who may, by any acts of violence, or even of intimidation, endeavour to prevent the arrest of the principals.

6th. When a felony has been committed, any person who witnesses it may immediately raise his neighbours and pursue the felons, and the pursuers may justify the use of all such means as a constable might use. If they overtake the parties, they should bid or signify to them to surrender; if they resist, or attempt to resist, the persons pursuing may use such force as is necessary; and if the pursued fly, and cannot otherwise be taken, the pursuers may then use similar means.[41]

To investigate further the policy and intention of the colonial government, it is necessary to examine the three steps taken between April 1828 and October 1830 that aimed to intensify the pressure on the Aborigines: firstly, the decision in April 1828 to demand that the tribes remove from, or be driven out of, the settled districts; secondly, the declaration of martial law later that year over the same area to enforce the earlier injunction; and thirdly, the organisation of the Black Line in October and November 1830, when 2200 well-armed men tramped across Tasmania from north to south making for the peninsulas in the far south-east corner.

The governor was convinced by the end of 1827 that he had to do something, given the number of settlers killed in the spring of that year. In a dispatch to the Colonial Office in January 1828 he explained that the insurgent tribes had 'latterly assumed so formidable an appearance, and perpetrated such repeated outrages', that he had been 'pressingly called upon by the settlers' to free them from these 'troublesome assailants'. He still hoped to achieve a negotiated settlement that would allow him to provide the Aborigines with 'some remote corner of the island, which would be strictly reserved for them'. He realised that such a plan faced great difficulties, but believed that it was

> but justice, to make the attempt, for notwithstanding the clamour and urgent appeals which are now made to me for the adoption of harsh measures, I cannot divest myself of the consideration that all aggression originated with the white inhabitants, and that therefore much ought to be endured in return before the blacks are treated as an open and accredited enemy of the government.[42]

His language was tougher in internal memos written to his officials. In one, dated 30 November 1827, he wrote that it had become a 'measure of indispensable necessity' to drive the 'black savages' from the settled districts and indicated that more troops would be sent into the country to enforce the policy.[43]

But the problem still perplexed him. There were no easy answers 'unless a war of extirpation is sanctioned', but nothing, he emphasised, other than 'absolute and inescapable necessity will induce me to authorize or sanction'.[44]

When writing to his superiors in Downing Street of his decision to force the tribes out of the settled districts, Arthur spent more time explaining his motivation. He referred to the 'painful necessity' of adopting some 'decided measures to suppress the increasing spirit of resentment' manifested by the 'coloured inhabitants of this colony' and the difficulty he felt in determining the measures it would be most advisable to pursue. He continued:

> It gives me great concern to state that the animosity of these wretched people is in no degree abated, and that their increasing predatory incursions upon the settled districts, which are accompanied with the perpetration of frequent barbarous murders, have overcome my reluctance to proceed to any coercive measures against them.
>
> The subject has undergone several days' anxious deliberation and discussion in the Executive Council; and having examined all such persons as are competent to give information, I am at length convinced of the absolute necessity of separating the Aborigines altogether from the white inhabitants, and of removing the former entirely from the settled districts, until their habits shall become more civilized.
>
> The proclamation which I have issued, with the unanimous advice of the Council, fully explains the origin and progress of the unhappy feeling which exists, and the measures directed for the purpose of averting its further fatal consequences.
>
> It is a subject most painful under every consideration; we are undoubtedly the first aggressors, and the desperate characters amongst the prisoner population, who have from time to time absconded into the woods, have no doubt committed the greatest outrages upon the natives, and these ignorant beings, incapable of discrimination, are now filled with enmity and revenge against the whole body of white inhabitants. It is perhaps at this time in vain to trace the cause of the evil which exists; my duty is plainly to remove its effects; and there does not appear any practicable method of accomplishing this measure, short of entirely prohibiting the Aborigines from entering the settled districts, a measure, however, which you may be assured shall be carried into execution without the least avoidable harshness.
>
> I have long indulged the expectation that kindness and forbearance would have brought about something like a reconciliation, but the repeated

murders which have been committed have so greatly inflamed the passions of the settlers, that petitions and complaints have been presented from every part of the Colony, and the feeling of resentment now runs so high that further forbearance would be totally indefensible.

My intention was to have given up one district to the Natives from their favourite haunts, but, beyond this, there is no occasion that His Majesty's Government should be apprehensive, and I do not even yet resign all hope of pacifying those angry feelings which are at present but too evident on both sides.

His Majesty's instructions command that every measure shall be resorted to for the instruction and civilization of the Natives; may I therefore beg to be honoured with your commands, whether, in promoting this attempt, I am to consider myself authorized to afford some temporary relief in food and clothing, which I fear affords the only prospect of quieting a tribe of savages, and may perhaps be absolutely necessary for their support beyond the settled districts.[45]

The policy adopted in April 1828 had little effect. Violence escalated during the year, leading to the decision to declare martial law over the settled district. This, the solicitor-general explained, placed the Aborigines 'within the prescribed limits on the footing of open enemies of the king, in state of actual warfare against him'.[46]

In justifying the decision, Arthur referred to the instructions he had received from Darling in 1825 concerning the need to 'oppose force by force'. He read them to his executive council on the eve of the decision to declare martial law and quoted them again in his next dispatch to the Colonial Office.[47] The council agreed that the measure was the only means of affording to the king's subjects protection against the atrocities of the Aborigines. It was hoped that it would be the means of 'putting a speedy stop, without much bloodshed, to the lawless warfare' between the Aborigines and the frontier settlers.[48] The council felt the 'deepest regret in advising these measures', but found themselves compelled to do so by 'an inevitable necessity'. 'To inspire them with terror', the councillors declared, 'will be found the only effectual means of security for the future'.[49]

At the same time, the government spoke of restraint. In his official proclamation Arthur urged on his troops and their civilian auxiliaries a measured response, declaring:

> But I do, nevertheless, hereby strictly order, enjoin and command, that the actual use of arms be in no case resorted to if the Natives can by other means be induced or compelled to retire into the places and portions of this island hereinbefore excepted from the operation of martial law; that bloodshed be checked as much as possible; that any tribes which may surrender themselves up shall be treated with every degree of humanity; and that defenceless women and children be invariably spared.[50]

The proclamation was a public document prepared for a wide audience and may therefore be viewed with suspicion. However, similar sentiments were expressed in the confidential instruction delivered to the military officers out in the field, who were told:

> You will understand that the Government puts forth its strength on this occasion by no means whatever with a view of seeking the destruction of the Aborigines; on the contrary, it is hoped, by energetic and decisive measures, and by punishing the leaders in the atrocities which have been perpetrated, that an end will be put to that lawless and cruel warfare which is now carrying on, and which must terminate in the annihilation of the Natives.

The officers were urged to see the necessity of conducting all proceedings in their respective districts 'with moderation and humanity' and to provide the governor with weekly reports of operations, which should include 'very *minutely*' what steps had been taken for 'opening a conciliatory intercourse and arrangements with the tribes . . .'[51]

FIVE

TASMANIA: THE BLACK LINE AND WYBALENNA

NEITHER TERROR NOR conciliatory intercourse had much effect on the level of violence. Thus the third and most dramatic policy decision was made: to organise a massive armed sweep across the centre of the colony. The Black Line has loomed so large in accounts of the Tasmanian genocide that it is necessary to consider it in detail.

In the relevant dispatch to London, Arthur emphasised that his primary object was not to kill the Aborigines despite the size of the well-armed force. It was the government's earnest desire 'rather to capture the savages, and place them in some situation of security, where they can neither receive nor inflict injury, than destroy their lives'. The Line was designed to capture them with the least possible destruction of life, or to drive them into Tasman's Peninsula.[1]

Given the known views of the Colonial Office, it is only to be expected that Arthur would emphasise in his dispatch his earnest desire to avoid bloodshed. A better idea of the governor's intentions emerges from the private correspondence sent out to magistrates and military officers. In a government order issued on 9 September, the colonial secretary, John Burnett, observed that should success crown the contemplated measure, the governor earnestly enjoined that 'the utmost tenderness and humanity may be manifested towards whatever Natives may be captured'.[2] On 22 September, when the final plans were being put in place, Arthur took the opportunity

> of again enjoining the whole community to bear in mind, that the object in view is not to injure or destroy the unhappy savages, against whom these movements will be directed, but to capture and raise them in the scale of civilization, by placing them under the immediate control of a competent establishment, from whence they will not have it in their power to escape and where they themselves will no longer be subject to the miseries of perpetual warfare, or to the privations which the extension of the settlement would progressively entail upon them . . .[3]

More detail about policy emerges from the letters sent out to minor officials and prominent settlers in the countryside. The police magistrate at Oatlands, Thomas Anstey, wrote to James Cox of *Clarendon* that while 'one or two parties may fall in with the Tribes and destroy some of them', experience had shown that nothing but 'a very large force is capable of *capturing* them which is the object everyone must have most at heart'.[4] Burnett wrote to the police magistrate in Launceston, urging that nothing should be omitted 'to cultivate and promote a good understanding with the friendly natives' north of the town, who were to be by no means injured or in any way molested.[5] In a memo to the magistrates, Burnett explained that much depended on them to enjoin the assigned servants to be orderly and sober and to point out to them that the object 'is to capture and civilize the wretched Natives and not destroy them'.[6]

There is little in Arthur's public or private papers to indicate what he was thinking as the Line moved slowly towards the south-east corner of the colony. The closest we can come to an understanding of the personal views of the senior officials is in the letters written by Colonial Secretary Burnett to Arthur while Arthur was out in the field directing operations between 15 October and 16 November 1830. A striking aspect of the letters is Burnett's obvious anxiety about the outcome of the Line and his uncertainty as to how it would turn out.

'We are all here as you may well believe', he wrote on 15 October, 'on the tip-toe for intelligence from the "seat of war".' As nothing of an authentic nature had reached Hobart, 'a thousand vague and absurd reports of Battles fought and captives taken' were in circulation.[7] The surface anxiety reflected a deep ambivalence on Burnett's part about the policy, the outcome of the Line, or the Aborigines themselves, who were described variously in letters written only days apart as 'unfortunate natives', 'poor savages' and 'wretched savages'. His swirling emotions were expressed in a letter of 18 October, thanking Arthur for the first news from the Line, and the proceedings

> against the unfortunate Natives, for whom I must ever entertain sentiments of commiseration, and hence arises the intense interest which I take in the present operations, the final result I look for with such anxiety.[8]

On 20 October Burnett referred to 'this most desirable object', the reconciliation of 'these unfortunate beings to the white inhabitants'.[9] Three days later he told Arthur that in Hobart every person 'seems to take the greatest interest in, and to feel the most intense anxiety respecting the present operation'. He was happy to hear that there was still a good chance of succeeding in the capture of the most 'daring and inveterate Tribe of Aborigines'.[10] By 4 November he observed that the feeling of intense interest and anxiety for the success of the venture was universal in the town. It had naturally increased as the operation appeared to be drawing to a crisis. 'God grant', he wrote, 'that your Excellency's exertions to drive these unfortunate and wretched beings' across Tasmania would prove successful and that 'you may be spared the lamentable and dreadful alternative of putting them to death'.[11]

A week later Burnett reported a conversation with the tough frontiersman John Batman, who had shocked the studious civil servant with stories about the boldness of the Aborigines and their knowledge of firearms. The exchange led him to fear that:

> Should the present enterprize fail, that the only chance of safety or security to the Settlers and white inhabitants will arise from the utter extermination of these wretched savages, who I greatly fear in that event will be hunted on all sides like Wild Beasts; an alternative too dreadful to be thought of, and whence I pray God in his infinite Mercy, will yet interpose to avert. But self-preservation is certainly the first law of nature, and it can hardly be expected that the white inhabitants of this Fine Island will much longer patiently endure the aggressions of these unfortunate people, and in that case, they will most assuredly be picked off one by one, till not a vestige of the original owners and occupiers of the Soil will remain.[12]

Arthur himself reflected on the outcome of the Line on 20 November when success appeared unlikely. He wrote to Sir George Murray:

> I cannot . . . say that I am sanguine of success, since their cunning and intelligence are remarkable; but whilst I hope His Majesty's Government will approve of my having omitted no measures which had a tendency to conciliate, or to preserve the lives of these savages, I am sure it will always be a matter of consolation to the Government of the Colony, and to its respectable inhabitants, that we have made every effort in our power to save the aboriginal race from being exterminated . . .[13]

Why, then, have historians and scholars of genocide so often declared that the colonial government of Governor Arthur was guilty of what Robert Hughes called the only true genocide in English colonial history? The main events of Tasmanian history seem to confirm the suspicions of the scholars. The colony's Aboriginal population declined rapidly after the first settlement in 1803 and it is well known that Trugernanna, the so-called last full-blooded person, died in 1876. For many years the Tasmanians were thought to be a unique race unrelated to the Australian

Aborigines, and this gave added poignancy to Trugernanna's passing.

Another feature of Tasmanian history is that it is remarkably well documented and that the government itself played a major role in the most significant developments relating to the demographic disaster. There is hard evidence of a decline from perhaps 1500 indigenous Tasmanians at the beginning of the Black War in 1824, to about 350 in 1831. As well, the high death rate at Wybalenna on Flinders Island is well known, with numbers falling from about 220 in 1833 to 46 in 1847. In the first period, many Aborigines must have been killed by British troops, official para-military roving parties or armed settlers encouraged by the government to defend themselves. Many others may have succumbed to the extreme rigours of guerilla war and the pressure exerted by the military campaign waged at the direction of Governor Arthur. Writing of the survivors of the Black War, the nineteenth-century historian James Bonwick observed:

> They had fought for the soil, and were vanquished. They had lost fathers, brothers, and sons in war. Their mothers, wives and daughters, harassed by continued alarms, worn by perpetual marches, enfeebled by want and disease, had sunk down one by one to die in the forest, leaving but a miserable remnant. Their children had been sacrificed to the cruel exaction of patriotism, and had perished of cold, hunger and fatigue.[14]

But what of genocide? How can the concept be related to the settlers, the Colonial Office and the Tasmanian administration of Governor Arthur?

During the 1820s it was, as illustrated above, clearly quite common for the settlers to discuss the extermination of the Aborigines, whether they favoured such an eventuality, were horrified by it or just considered it inevitable. We have no way of knowing how many settlers were what George Augustus Robinson called 'extirpationists' and how many others opposed them. The leading scholar of the history of the Tasmanian Aborigines, N. J. B. Plomley, believed that in the 1820s most colonists were 'extirpationists at heart'.[15] What is certainly true is that prominent settlers felt no compunction about publicly expressing their genocidal desires and intentions and apparently had no concern about courting public disapproval or social ostracism by advocating extermination. They clearly felt no need to guard their tongue or modify their language. Frontier stockmen and shepherds were even less constrained. Robinson interviewed a shepherd in the north-west of the colony who 'seemed to glory in the act and said he would shoot them whenever he met them'.[16] Fellow frontiersmen declared they would 'shoot them whenever they may find them'.[17]

It is true that when educated settlers spoke in public or wrote to the government they often qualified their advocacy of extermination with comments like 'horrible as the idea is', it was 'dreadful to contemplate' or a 'dreadful alternative'. When Alfred Stephen spoke to the public meeting in Hobart he referred to the ongoing guerilla war and said that his preference was to capture the Aborigines rather than destroy them. There was no suggestion that he thought they should be killed if they surrendered.

The Colonial Office, as we have seen, had thoughts about extermination. Sir George Murray feared that the rapid decline of population presaged extinction 'at no distant period' but warned the colonial government to eschew any line of conduct that might hasten that end. It was a most unusual dispatch; there is none other like it in the whole correspondence between the Colonial Office and the Australian colonies (although London bureaucrats often voiced their dark fears about genocide in their intra-office memos). It suggested that Murray, or his officials, had serious doubts about the intentions of Arthur's administration. Whether they had received unofficial news of Tasmanian events from returning settlers or visitors to the antipodes is impossible to determine, but clearly the imperial government was determined that the responsibility for the feared extinction would be sheeted home to the colonists and their government.

Imperial responsibility could not, in fact, be shed so easily. The tragic events in Tasmania in the 1820s had their genesis in the colonising venture itself. Governors like Arthur and Darling were told to treat the Aborigines well while presiding over the rapid increase in immigration, both bond and free, and the corresponding expansion of settlement into Aboriginal territory without a treaty, negotiation or purchase. The inevitable indigenous resistance provided justification for the colonial office to instruct its governors in 1825 to make war on the tribes as though they were agents of a foreign state. The imperial government sanctioned war but not genocide and in doing so ensured that responsibility for the ensuing bloodshed was shipped out from London to Hobart and Sydney.

What of Governor Arthur and his administration? Did they pursue policies that had the avowed or secret object of 'the extinction of the native race'? Were they guilty of what we now call genocide, the intention to destroy the Tasmanian Aborigines?

Arthur was a professional soldier. He believed he was engaged in warfare, in a war 'of the most dreadful kind',[18] which presented enormous difficulties to the government. The Aborigines were elusive; they were experts in the bush who could attack isolated Europeans and disappear into the mountains before they could be pursued, making it impossible even to find any large body of tribesmen to attack and defeat. There were no forts to besiege, villages to attack, crops to burn or wells to poison. Nor did there appear to be any chiefs or leaders with whom to negotiate. If Arthur and his military officers could not create conditions where they could employ their great superiority in both manpower and firepower to inflict a decisive defeat on the enemy, they would endeavour to drive them away from the contested territory. In many ways, Arthur's response to the Aboriginal insurgency was more measured and gradual than his ruthless and decisive crushing of the bushranging gangs that had ranged the colony during 1825 and 1826.

How far was Arthur willing to go to defeat the enemy? Ideally he would have sought his ends without bloodshed. He wrote many official instructions urging his subordinates to attempt to conciliate and persuade. However, there is no doubt he intended to use whatever force was required to crush the indigenous insurgency. In November 1827 he explained that he would not authorise 'a war of extirpation' unless there was a situation of 'absolute and inescapable necessity'. So we know from his own words that Arthur had at least contemplated such a war – but did 'absolute and inescapable necessity' ever confront him?

We must remember that a year after this statement the secretary of state sternly warned Arthur that any plan which sought the extinction of the native race would leave an indelible stain on the British government (and, no doubt, on the record of the culpable official). The warning must have alerted Arthur to the growing strength of humanitarian ideas in Britain in the late 1820s and the need to take heed of them. He was an able and ambitious official who was keenly aware of the importance of maintaining his reputation in Downing Street. Even so, the Black Line could have ended in bloodshed. Presumably Arthur was willing to accept that risk – although the very size of the operation was probably designed to overawe the Aborigines and thereby lessen the likelihood of conflict. Arthur may well have seen the situation in the same way as his colonial secretary, Burnett, who hoped the Line would drive the tribes across Tasmania and avoid direct confrontation.

In his own justification, Arthur argued that, given the intensity of the conflict in the late 1820s and the deep hatreds generated, the settlers would eventually wipe out the Aborigines of central Tasmania. He returned to the same argument when justifying the Black Line, which he said was launched to impose a peace, put down insurgency and 'save the Aboriginal race from being exterminated'.[19]

Members of the executive council made similar observations on the eve of the Black Line. The relevant minute read:

[The Council] hopes and believes that if a sufficient force can be thus collected, the expulsion of the Natives may be effected at the expense of little bloodshed; and even if it should cost more lives than the Council antici-

pates, it is a measure dictated not less by humanity than by necessity, since
it is calculated to bring to a decisive issue a state of warfare which there
seems no hope of ending by other means, and which, if much longer
continued, the Council feels will become a war of annihilation.[20]

The official Aborigines Committee took the view that without
government action the colonists would 'individually or in small bodies
take violent steps against the Aborigines'. It was an eventuality that
committee members could not 'contemplate the possibility [sic] without
horror', but at the same time they were convinced that many colonists
welcomed the prospect of a genocidal campaign.[21]

Whatever one makes of these justifications by the governor and senior
members of his administration, there is no doubt that, left to themselves,
the settlers would have eventually wiped out the tribes of central
Tasmania. By the late 1820s they outnumbered the Aborigines by twenty
to one, and rapidly expanding settlement was increasing the pressure on
land and resources. By the time the Black Line advanced across the
colony, Aboriginal numbers were greatly reduced. One of the reasons
for the spectacular failure of the Line – only two Aborigines were
captured – was that there were so few people left. In 1831, when the
remnant of the much-feared Big River and Oyster Bay tribes surrendered to Robinson, there were only twenty-six of them left – sixteen
men, nine women and one child.

A distinctive feature of the Tasmanian experience was the central role
played by the government, which appears to modern scholars to bring it
within the range of systematic and well-planned genocides. But an often-
overlooked aspect of Tasmanian history is that Arthur was always acutely
aware of the fact that he governed a penal colony and that most of the
workforce in the rural areas was made up of assigned servants still under
sentence. He dreaded the prospect of armed convicts engaging in uncontrolled skirmishing with the Aborigines. He was unwilling to let the frontier
shepherds and stockmen fight it out with their tribal adversaries: convicts
with guns in their hands could easily cohere into bushranging gangs.

So if conflict was inevitable, it was essential to keep control of it and ensure that military officers, magistrates and prominent settlers managed all local operations and continued 'to enforce a due degree of subordination on the Convicts'.[22] In a circular to his magistrates in November 1828 Arthur observed:

> You will, therefore, see the necessity of regulating all proceedings in your district, as far as possible, by principles of moderation and humanity; and you will perceive the advantage and propriety of consultation and frequent communication with all the magistrates and respectable inhabitants, so as to form a combined plan of operation, and to leave nothing that is avoidable in the hands of undirected convicts, or other unauthorized persons.[23]

Whatever is said about the Black Line, the fact is that it failed. It did not effect the removal of the tribes from central Tasmania, nor did it bring an end to conflict. But the events of 1828–30 do provide material for a reconsideration of some of the main themes found in the contemporary literature on genocide and related phenomena.

The attempt, by various means, to sweep the settled districts clear of the resident Aboriginal tribes has similarities with the modern practice of forced removal of peoples and ethnic cleansing, recently defined as the 'planned and deliberate removal from a certain territory of an undesirable population distinguished by one or more characteristics such as ethnicity, religion, race, class or sexual preferences'.[24] But it is important to emphasise that the Line was only directed against the tribes in the central districts and not those in the north-west, north-east, west and far south of the colony.

What of genocide? Perhaps the most relevant area of study to pursue is the relationship between genocide and warfare. One problem with much of the international literature concerning Tasmania is that most writers appear to be unaware that at the critical period in question the colony

was immersed in fierce guerilla warfare. Lacking this essential infor-
mation, the writers cannot account for the actions of the colonial
government beyond assuming that there was a brutal but generalised
desire to get rid of the Aborigines. Linked to this failure to understand
settler motivation is an entirely patronising view of the Aborigines as
helpless but pathetic victims of the colonists' murderous impulses or the
violence of psychologically disturbed or even psychopathic convicts.
People who displayed a 'haunting naivete', who lived like 'children in the
woods', could scarcely be seen as being effective adversaries of professional British soldiers who gave as good as they got.

The reality was quite different. For five years the colony was seriously disrupted by Aboriginal aggression. As Arthur explained in a
dispatch to London, the guerilla war was a 'heavy calamity upon the
Colony'; it was a subject that, he explained, 'wholly engrosses and fills
my mind with painful anxiety'.[25] The settlers in the countryside lived in
high anxiety for years on end. As the Aborigines Committee reported
in March 1830:

> They continue to occupy and ravage, beyond the reach of control, and in
> defiance of the orders and efforts of Government . . . Since the commence-
> ment of the present year an unparalleled series of devastations has marked
> their passage through the country.[26]

After listing all the recent attacks, committee members had no hesitation
in expressing their persuasion

> that a sentiment of alarm pervades the minds of the settlers throughout the
> Island, and that the total ruin of every establishment is but too certainly to
> be apprehended, unless immediate means can be devised for suppressing
> the system of aggression under which so many are at this time suffering,
> and of which all are in dread that they may themselves become the victims.[27]

The Tasmanian government was at war with the local Aborigines during the late 1820s and early 1830s, operating under official

instructions that permitted the authorities to oppose force with force. Many settlers undoubtedly were extirpationists at heart, but it is not clear if this was true of the officials and military officers. Whether Governor Arthur strayed over the unmarked border between warfare and genocide cannot be answered with any certainty. As always, it depends on what is meant by genocide. It is clear that Arthur was determined to defeat the Aborigines and secure the permanent expropriation of their land, but there is little evidence to suggest that he wanted to reach beyond that objective and destroy the Tasmanian race in whole or in part. After all, he had been specifically warned against such action by his superiors in London and carrying it out would serve no particular purpose.

In her book *Genocide: A Sociological Perspective*, Fein observes that a major issue in the study of genocide is the question of intent and that this is often problematic when killings occurred during war and colonisation. In order to untangle the interrelated phenomena of war and genocide, she suggests that were the victims of war to surrender, their killing should cease, whereas 'the surrender of victims in genocidal situations does not avoid their mass murder but expedites it'.[28]

Between 1830 and 1834 the surviving Tasmanians were removed from the mainland to Wybalenna, a settlement on Flinders Island in Bass Strait. What happened to them there must now be considered in order further to explore the question of genocide and Tasmanian history. Did the move expedite their mass murder? Did they retain the right to existence?

The most important fact about Wybalenna was that it was a place of death. As stated earlier, Aboriginal numbers declined from about 220 in 1833 to 46 in 1847. By then, any hope of demographic recovery had passed. The question that must be asked is: Did the Tasmanian government intend this outcome? Was it a consequence of neglect? Could it be construed as the final act of genocide?

Many writers have thought so over the years. Hughes characterised Flinders Island as 'a concentration camp where genocide was committed'.[29] Diamond believed that the government deliberately neglected the settlement and reduced expenditure 'in the hope that the natives would die out',[30] while Morris observed that they were taken to Flinders Island to die like 'unwanted old relatives consigned to an institution'.[31] Mr Justice Wilcox took a similar view in his judgement in *Nulyarimma v. Thompson*. When considering the question of genocide in Australian history, he thought that some of the destruction clearly fell into this category. A 'notable example' was the 'rounding-up of the remaining Tasmanian Aboriginals in the 1830s, and their removal to Flinders Island'.[32]

Given the importance attached to the question of intent, it is necessary to consider the motives of the government in establishing Wybalenna and their expectations of what would happen to the transplanted Aboriginal community.

The idea of removing the Aborigines from mainland Tasmania to an island in Bass Strait had been advocated by numerous settlers from the start of the Black War in 1826. The governor was initially opposed to the idea, observing in January 1828:

> Not to mention the extreme difficulty of this scheme, nothing short of the last necessity could tolerate so great an aggravation of their injuries, as they would unquestionably consider removing them from their native tracts.[33]

However, removal became a serious option after the failure of the Black Line and was discussed at length by the executive council in February 1831. There were two contending views. George Augustus Robinson cast doubt on the possibility of negotiating a settlement with 'their Chiefs' to partition Tasmania because they did not have sufficient power over the tribes to enforce obedience. He was of the opinion that

> the Natives generally would not object to be removed to an island in Basses Straits [sic], and . . . it would be humane policy towards them, as [I feel] satisfied the government can never sufficiently protect them from the outrages the sealers and runaway convicts inflict upon the tribes.

Robinson assured the senior officials that if the Tasmanians were placed on an island they would not feel themselves imprisoned 'or pine away in consequence of the restraint'.[34] His views were directly challenged by the chief justice, John Pedder, who felt he could not recommend the adoption of measures 'tending to induce the Natives' to consent to expatriation or imprisonment, for

> notwithstanding Mr Robinson's opinion to the contrary, that, however carefully these people might be supplied with food, they would soon begin to pine away when they found their situation one of hopeless imprisonment . . .[35]

The governor felt the risk was worth it, for even if they 'should pine away' in the manner suggested by the chief justice, it was better that they die in exile 'whilst every act of kindness [was] manifested towards them' than that they should 'fall a sacrifice' in fighting in the bush.[36]

Of more direct relevance to the present investigation is what the government officials did and said once the community had been established in Bass Strait. Having been warned by his chief justice about the likely consequences of forced expatriation, Arthur became increasingly anxious to keep the exiles alive and well. He wrote to the first superintendent of the settlement, Lieutenant William Darling, to explain that he had 'no wish more sincerely at heart than that every care should be afforded these unfortunate people'.[37]

For his part, the lieutenant strongly promoted the Aboriginal cause and believed that, while the cost of the settlement was a heavy burden, it was evident that the 'poor savages being deprived of their own country must be maintained by the colony and rendered as happy and comfortable as it is possible to make them'.[38] He was fully aware of the great brutality suffered by the remnant tribes and believed that the Bass Strait islands were a secure asylum. 'Under the present circumstances', he wrote to the governor, no more humane measure could be adopted than that of placing them on this island, that is, if proper means be taken to civilize and improve them, and to render them contented and happy.

Should this poor remnant of the original inhabitants of Van Diemen's Land be thus rescued from destruction, as it were, to show the world that they are possessed of intellect and feeling equally with those whose skin is of a lighter colour, it will surely confer a lustre on the present Government of the Colony . . .[39]

The governor's attitude to the settlement was most fully outlined in several interviews he had with Robinson in May 1836. Robinson noted in his diary that Arthur 'seemed deeply interested about the settlement'. He granted all the assistance Robinson asked for and 'begged I would omit nothing which I conceived necessary for the comfort and good of the aborigines'.[40] The governor said that if in the future there was any difficulty about receiving supplies, Robinson should 'write to him direct'. Reacting to news of shortages on the island, Arthur wrote a memo to his officials requiring them to notify the departments concerned that he was 'particularly anxious' that provisions for Flinders Island be dispatched 'with utmost regularity'. He reminded his officials that this request had 'frequently been most expressly directed'[41] and told Robinson that the Aborigines 'were not to want for anything'.[42] Above all else, Arthur 'begged and entreated' that the superintendent would 'use every endeavour to prevent the race from becoming extinct'.[43]

Similar views were expressed by the senior military officer, Major Thomas Ryan, who was sent to Flinders Island in March 1836 to report on conditions at the settlement. He found that it had suffered from 'disgraceful neglect' and informed Robinson that his wish was to 'work hand and heart with you for the preservation of these poor people'.[44] He hoped that a new era was dawning for 'this interesting, this wronged, and feeble people', emphasising that fresh meat and pure water were indispensable 'if the propagation of these people is desirable'. If that was the wish of the government, it was 'our bounded duty to provide all the means that are in our possession for the accomplishment of so desirable an end'.[45]

Later in the history of the settlement, officials were still making the same sort of commitment to the Aboriginal cause. In 1847 the superintendent of Wybalenna, Dr Henry Jeanneret, concluded his annual report with the declaration that he wished

> to preserve this remnant of the race as a palpable demonstration of the readiness and even anxiety of civilized and Christian man to remedy and repair the evils perpetrated by his progress.[46]

Later in 1847, when the Colonial Office recommended the return of the surviving Aborigines to mainland Tasmania, Governor William Denison wrote that he believed it was due 'to the former owners of the soil that they should be carefully tended and kindly treated' and if the race 'were to become extinct' it was important that the result 'ought not to be accelerated by any positive acts of government'.[47]

Despite the neglect and inefficiency of the Tasmanian administration, it was clear that the intention was that Wybalenna become home to a permanent population, with buildings and equipment commensurate with that intention. Robinson was determined to build in brick and in less than three months 12 000 bricks had been made on the settlement. Archaeologists who excavated the site in 1972 recorded that the houses were

> extremely well built, with lime wash over brick and limestone and carefully made and laid bricks. Glass was found from windows, lead from door fittings, brass door handles and washers, and iron pothooks in the fireplaces.[48]

A vast range of commodities was dispatched to the island to equip the community fully. Historian John West observed in 1852 that Wybalenna was furnished:

with every article of domestic use, far more numerous than usually fall to the lot of the English cottager, and which to an Irish peasant, would suggest the idea of shop keeping.[49]

Robinson asked for and got the convicts he required to work at the settlement, including many tradesmen who were in great demand elsewhere in the colony. During the second half of 1836 he recorded the arrival of two batches of assigned servants. In June, for example, the island greeted a ploughman, shepherd, gardener, farm labourer, carpenter, bricklayer, shoemaker and dispenser. There was a larger and more diverse draft at the end of the year, including a baker, another shoemaker, a brickmaker and bricklayer, a boatman, a mason, a carpenter, a pit-sawyer and top-sawyer, another ploughman, a butcher, a plasterer, a seaman, a blacksmith, a water-carter and a bullock-driver.[50] Wybalenna was thus by far the best-equipped and most lavishly staffed Aboriginal institution in the Australian colonies in the nineteenth century.

Expenditure on the establishment declined over time, but not as quickly as the population. There is no evidence to support Diamond's contention that the population was deliberately reduced in the hope that the Aborigines would die out. Though it is difficult to draw definite conclusions, it seems that the Aborigines at Wybalenna were better provided for than other groups dependent on the government. In the 1840s the colony's orphans cost the government 7 pence a day, infirm and destitute paupers 8 pence, convicts 10 pence and hospital-bound paupers 1 shilling. The Aborigines cost between 1/3d and 1/5d a day and this figure would have been considerably higher if the settlement had been charged for the labour of the large convict workforce that kept the community running. The convicts and Aborigines received similar rations of meat, flour, biscuits, tea and sugar, but unlike the felons, the Aborigines were able to supplement their diet with a range of shellfish from the seashore and wallaby caught on hunting expeditions.

Overriding every other aspect of life on Flinders Island was the endless saga of sickness, death and mourning. The Aborigines had little resistance to the bacteria and viruses brought by the Europeans, and pneumonia and other respiratory diseases were the main cause of death. Many writers have suggested that Flinders Island was a particularly unhealthy environment, but one of the medical officers who worked there judged it more salubrious than mainland Tasmania – and so it proved for the convicts, despite their hard regimen of work and discipline. Between September 1833 and May 1837 only one of the seventy convicts died of disease. In the same period forty Aborigines – men, women and children – succumbed.

The high death rate was due to factors largely beyond the control or understanding of the European staff. With a resident surgeon for most of the period, the community had far better access to professional medical help than the great majority of settlers on mainland Tasmania, although the standard treatments of bleeding and purging were totally futile and even counterproductive.

There is no evidence to suggest that the colonial officials at Flinders Island or on mainland Tasmania were anything other than distressed by the constant deaths. In December 1835 Robinson wrote in his journal:

> The aborigines, poor people, evince great fortitude under these awful dispensations. It is an appalling sight to view the mounds of earth now before us where the people are buried, as they are single graves. Each one reminds us that the body of a native lies there. This is their repository of the dead – no white man lies here. These are the remains of persons once animated as we are but now the crimson fluid ceases to circulate in their veins . . . of all ages and sexes, of all ranks and degrees of the aboriginal inhabitants, but alas no mixture of colour. These numerous graves contain only bodies of aborigines.[51]

There is little evidence that the Aborigines 'pined away'. They pleased themselves, refusing to work, demanding better conditions and rations, coming and going as they wished and often spending long periods out in the bush on hunting expeditions. They regarded the settlement as theirs and the clothes and rations as mere tokens in return for the loss of their land. They were exiles, but were far from being prisoners — or inmates of a concentration camp. When they sent a petition to Queen Victoria in 1846 complaining about the behaviour of Dr Jeanneret, they described themselves as the 'free Aborigines Inhabitants of Van Diemen's Land now living upon Flinders Island'.[52]

In the draft convention put together by the UN secretary-general, it was determined that in cases where victims were placed in concentration camps with an annual death rate of 30 to 40 per cent, the intention to commit genocide was unquestionable. Clearly the death rate on Flinders Island puts it well within the range of such death camps, but there is no available evidence at all to suggest that it was the intention of the colonial government to effect the extinction of the Tasmanians. But the question of genocide must now be addressed in relation to the history of the relations between European settlers and Aborigines on mainland Australia.

SIX

THE IMPENDING CATASTROPHE

IN 1830 THE COLONIAL OFFICE warned Governor Arthur against pursuing policies which had as their avowed or secret objective the extinction of the Tasmanian Aborigines. Within a few years the same colonial officials were expressing their private fears that the settlers on mainland Australia, right across the vast pastoral frontier of the Murray–Darling basin, were bent on the same project.

While imperial government policy had become more solicitous of Aboriginal welfare during the early 1830s, the capacity of the Colonial Office to control events had greatly diminished as a result of the squatting movement, which saw the settlers push back the boundaries of occupation and take their sheep and cattle out into the sprawling hinterland of south-eastern Australia. Officials in both London and Sydney discussed the problems created by the dispersion of settlement in regular dispatches. In London they privately agonised about the fate of the Aborigines as their land became occupied by frontier squatters.

In 1839 Governor George Gipps explained to his superiors in London that it was too late to calculate the 'evils of dispersion' in New South Wales. All the power of government, he observed,

aided even by a Military force ten times greater than that which is maintained in the Colony, would not suffice to bring back within the limits of
our twenty counties the Flocks and Herds, which now stray hundreds of
miles beyond them . . .[1]

When Gipps' dispatch reached the Colonial Office it was read by the
under-secretary, James Stephen, who wrote a memo to his colleagues in
which he said that the problem of the squatting rush was one 'admitting
of none but a very imperfect solution' and would at no remote period
'set all legislation at defiance'. The problem, he judged, was

> how to provide for the Government of persons hanging on the Frontiers
> of vast pastoral country to which there is no known or assignable limit. The
> backwoodsmen of the United States have a great nation in their vicinity and
> from the nature of their agricultural pursuits are to some extent stationary
> in their habits. The Shepherds and Herdsmen of New South Wales must
> bear a greater resemblance to the Nomadic Tribes of Russia and Tartary,
> and must I apprehend ultimately become almost as lawless and migratory
> a Race. To coerce them by Statute of any kind would I should conceive prove
> in the result a vain undertaking.[2]

Among the problems created by the squatting rush was the inability
to control frontier violence or to provide any protection to the Aborigines.
Stephen realised that the situation was out of control. English acts of
parliament, he wrote, were 'rather flimsy contrivances'; over squatters of
bad character the law could have little power.[3] From Sydney, Governor
Gipps echoed these sentiments. All his government could do was to raise,
'in the name of justice and humanity', a voice in favour of 'our poor savage
fellow creatures, too feeble to be heard at such a distance'.[4]

As dispatch after dispatch from New South Wales arrived in London
with news of further conflict between encroaching settlers and resident
tribes, Stephen concluded that the Aborigines would be exterminated
and there was little the government could do to prevent the tragedy. He

expressed his fears in memos scribbled on the corners or on the backs of the dispatches written by Gipps between 1838 and 1842. They were confidential intra-office memos and little of their dark foreboding found its way into the dispatches written back to Australia or into any other public document. However, they are of great interest for the present investigation and need to be considered in some detail.

On a dispatch of April 1838 from Governor Gipps referring to conflict between a party led by Major Nunn and the Aborigines in northern New South Wales, Stephen wrote:

> The causes and consequences of this state of things are alike clear and irremediable nor do I suppose that it is possible to discover any method by which the impending catastrophe, namely the extermination of the Black Race, can long be averted.

The following year Stephen scrawled at the end of another dispatch from Gipps:

> The tendency of these collisions with the Blacks is unhappily too clear for doubt. They will ere long cease to be numbered amongst the Races of the Earth. I can imagine no law effective enough to avoid this result . . . All this is most deplorable but I fear it is also inevitable. The only chance of saving them from annihilation would consist in teaching them the art of war and supplying them with weapons and munitions – an act of suicidal generosity which of course cannot be practised.[5]

Commenting on a dispatch from Gipps of April 1841 that provided details of a clash between Aborigines and a party under the command of Major Lettsom on the Ovens River, Stephen wrote:

> I am more and more convinced that these evils are irremediable and that the extermination of the whole Race is no very remote event.[6]

A few months later the comment was similar and succinct. 'Extermination', he minuted, 'would soon take place'. It was 'very lamentable and the approaching catastrophe' was still more so. Yet he did not know what more could be done 'to avoid it than has already been attempted'.[7] On a dispatch of September 1841 with further reports of collisions on the frontier, Stephen observed that it was 'but one proof the more, that the aboriginal Race will disappear before the European Settlers'.[8]

When news reached London in 1843 of the closing of a mission near Geelong because of the rapid decline of the local Aboriginal population, Stephen returned to his well-worn theme. The most important statement was one relating to the 'rapid extinction of the Aboriginal race', a calamity that no human power could 'avert or mitigate'.[9]

For much of the time that Stephen was under-secretary of the Colonial Office (1836–47), he expressed a consistent view about relations between colonists and indigenes in New South Wales. He was convinced that the Aborigines were doomed to destruction. He no doubt appreciated the importance of disease, change of lifestyle and deprivation in furthering this process, but he constantly referred to the impact of frontier violence and the disproportionate deaths of blacks as opposed to whites. He was fully aware that much of the conflict arose from the rapid and uncontrolled occupation of Aboriginal land, but also pointed to psychological factors, to the presence of attitudes which today would be termed racist. For example, he referred to the

> hatred with which the white man regards the Black which resulted from fear – from the strong physical contrasts which intercept the sympathy which subsists between men of the same Race – from the consciousness of having done them great wrongs and from the desire to escape this painful reproach by laying the blame on the injured party.[10]

The views of James Stephen mattered at the time and they continue to be of interest. Although he had never set foot in Australia, he probably had a more comprehensive understanding of developments all over that continent than anyone in the antipodes. He read dispatches from the four colonies – New South Wales, Van Diemen's Land, South Australia and Western Australia – and was able to see Australian developments in the perspective of the empire as a whole. He had been associated with the Colonial Office, in one way or another, from 1813 and was undoubtedly one of the outstanding officials of the period, a measured, astute man who did not rush to judgement and brought much experience to his assessments of what was happening in New South Wales.

What Stephen said over and over again was that the frontier settlers were in the process of exterminating the Aborigines; they were guilty of what, since the 1940s, has been called genocide and that the government was powerless to stop them. This was an extraordinarily frank admission to come from the permanent head of the Colonial Office and has to carry considerable weight in any historical assessment of the question. Stephen clearly believed that the settlers had the psychological and emotional drive – the *dolus specialis* – to carry out genocide. He believed that his government was in the position of a powerless bystander – the situation described by the Venezuelan delegate to the Ad Hoc Committee on the Genocide Convention, Sr Perez Perozo, who referred to a 'weak Government unable to prevent the extermination of a group occupying a distant region'.[11]

If governments are the main agents of genocide – either by intent or inability to prevent it happening – then James Stephen provided us with a form of confession. He clearly felt, however, that the moral responsibility lay with the 'squatters of bad character', over whom the law had little power, rather than with the imperial government that had set the whole process of colonisation in motion.

But was there ever enough evidence to give substance to Stephen's confession and to conclude that genocide was perpetrated in New South Wales in the late 1830s and early 1840s?

There is no doubt that there was great loss of life among the Aboriginal tribes of south-eastern Australia between 1835 and 1850, coinciding with the occupation of the land in question by the squatters and their flocks and herds. We will never know how many people died at this time, nor the precise causes of death. Introduced diseases, disruption of traditional life and malnutrition would all have played a part. Rampant venereal infections greatly reduced the fertility of Aboriginal women, which curtailed the possibility of replacing those who died prematurely.

But many Aborigines also died in conflict with the Europeans. This conflict was at its height in the late 1830s and early 1840s and was apparent in all areas of new European settlement, from northern New South Wales and what was to become southern Queensland in a great arc through the Murray–Darling basin to the outskirts of Adelaide. Evidence about frontier conflict abounds and can be found in New South Wales and South Australian government reports, in dispatches to the Colonial Office, in newspapers published in Sydney, Adelaide, Melbourne, Maitland, Portland and Geelong, and in letters and books written by the settlers themselves and by visitors to the colonies.

Conflict was, then, widespread and resulted in considerable loss of Aboriginal life. But were the frontier settlers bent on the extermination of the Aborigines, as James Stephen feared?

It is certain that many colonists in New South Wales talked openly of extermination and extirpation in the 1830s and 1840s, just as their Tasmanian counterparts had done ten or so years earlier. Visitors from Britain were often horrified by the sentiments expressed publicly in the colonies. The Quaker missionary James Backhouse, who travelled widely in Australia during the 1830s, observed that:

> Persons who before they emigrated would have shuddered at the idea of murdering their fellow creatures, have, in many instances, wantonly taken the lives of the Aborigines. And many of those who have desired to cultivate a good feeling towards them, have found them such an annoyance, as to have their benevolent intentions superseded by a desire to have these hapless people removed out of the way.[12]

The Royal Navy captain, J. L. Stokes, had similar experiences to Backhouse while in the Australian colonies, observing that such was the 'perversion of feeling among a portion of the colonists' that they could not conceive how anyone could sympathise with 'the black race as their fellow man'. In theory and practice they regarded the Aborigines 'as wild beasts who it is lawful to extirpate'.[13]

The official Aboriginal Protectors who worked in what later became Victoria during the 1840s recorded many conversations in their letters and journals. William Thomas was greatly surprised soon after he had taken up his position when a Mr S___ said the Protectorate would do no good and that there would be no peace 'till the Blacks are extirpated'. In a letter a few months later he observed that the settlers in his district were, with some exceptions, 'averse to the Blacks almost to a spirit of extermination'.[14] One of the wealthiest squatters said to him:

> to go in search of them to pacify them I should not be able to get a single man to accompany me, but if I would go in search of them with the intent to exterminate them I would undertake that I could get 30 at least of men in the surrounding District who would willingly volunteer in the service.[15]

Thomas's colleagues reported like opinions. E. S. Parker observed that he had sought the views of the magistrates and leading settlers on the Wimmera and Glenelg rivers and discovered the most deadly feelings of animosity. His informants said the two races were incompatible and that half the blacks had to be shot.[16]

G. A. Robinson, who travelled widely around the frontier districts, recorded many similar comments in his journals. A prominent squatter, Mr H___, told him that it was necessary to use terror to keep the Aborigines in subjection and to 'punish them wholesale – that is by tribes and communities – if a tribe offended destroy the whole'. H___ declared that he believed 'they must be exterminated'.[17] A 'respectable' settler told Robinson that while he admitted the Aboriginal situation was a hard one and he would be sorry to see them injured, he thought that 'under all circumstances the sooner they are got rid of the better'.[18] On one occasion, Robinson met a party of settlers coming overland from New South Wales and got into conversation with them without telling them he was the Chief Protector of Aborigines. Their general feeling towards the blacks

> was hostile and . . . they openly asserted they would not hesitate to *get rid* of the blacks provided they could do it without detection . . . it was the most cruel that could be – they wished them to be burnt – hunted – drowned – speared – by any means they wished them got rid of.[19]

Other witnesses gave corresponding reports from other parts of the frontier. In December 1840 R. W. Newland observed that in the south-east of South Australia the general doctrine was 'kill and exterminate'.[20] A visitor to Gippsland in 1847 noted that at least some of the squatters wanted 'nothing more or less than their extermination'.[21] On the far side of the continent the editor of the *Perth Gazette* tried to take a more detached view of the matter. A crisis, he wrote, was at hand,

> and either the white inhabitants or the aborigines must obtain the mastery. Our position is by no means a peculiar one; all newly inhabited countries have the same trying ordeal to go through. Why, it is the order of nature that, as civilization advances, savage nations *must* be exterminated sooner or later. A few may be saved from the great mass and civilized; but their descendants, should they have any, soon lose their distinctive character, and become part of the new possessors of the soil.[22]

So was James Stephen right? Were the frontier settlers of New South Wales extirpationists? Clearly some of them were, and they said so publicly. Whether such people were in the majority in the bush, or in the colony as a whole, is impossible to say. But as we saw in Tasmania, it appeared to be acceptable to advocate extermination without fear of social opprobrium. The same views were expressed by prominent landowners and frontier shepherds, in remote bush huts and from the desks of colonial newspaper editors. A British military officer, Colonel G. C. Mundy, who travelled extensively in the colonies, was both shocked and surprised when 'men of station and cultivation' advocated indiscriminate retaliation against the Aborigines. A frontier settler told him he would shoot 'a blackfellow wherever he met him as he would a mad dog'.[23]

The explorer Edward Eyre was also struck by the 'recklessness' of conversation in the bush, where men thought as little of firing at a black 'as at a bird, and which makes the number they have killed, or the atrocities they have attended' a matter for a tale, or a jest or a boast 'at their pot house revelries'.[24]

There were always colonists who denounced indiscriminate killing and took up the Aboriginal cause in public and private. Even in the most troubled frontier regions there were squatters or officials who attempted to achieve reconciliation and who were appalled at the extent of the violence and at

the inhuman deeds of those whose motto is extermination, and whose atrocities have stained with *blood* – their unoffending *brothers' blood* – the page of colonial history.[25]

The army surgeon Thomas Bartlett, who was in New South Wales at the height of the squatting rush, concluded that there were two views 'diametrically opposed to each other' respecting the character of the Aboriginal population. One class of settler, which, he regretted, was numerous, maintained that the blacks were 'not entitled to be looked upon as fellow creatures' and in consequence adopted the harshest and most severe measures towards them. He was shocked to find that there were persons in 'respectable stations in society' who had the hardihood to defend the 'savage butcheries, by asserting [the Aborigines] resemble so many wild beasts' and that it was proper to 'destroy them accordingly'. But there were other colonists who saw things quite differently and who were 'deeply impressed with a sense of the sufferings' that had accrued to the Aboriginal inhabitants in consequence of the pressure of the Europeans.[26]

All of this does not advance the question of whether it is appropriate to employ the term genocide to the particular circumstances of New South Wales in the 1830s and 1840s. Indeed, it merely adds to the difficulties. In a situation where the government was not involved, how is it possible to judge the situation beyond saying that some colonists clearly were advocates and perhaps practitioners of extermination? What percentage of a population's involvement is required before the society itself can be considered to be genocidal? There were no organisations of extirpationists, no societies with genocide as their avowed objective, no institutional structures to further the cause. The most we can say is that in some parts of the colony, public opinion at least tolerated the killing of Aborigines in a sweeping and indiscriminate fashion and that witnesses were not forthcoming with evidence that would have facilitated prosecution.

Then there is the question of warfare. Many frontier settlers believed they were at war with the Aborigines. In northern New South Wales in the late 1830s the local police magistrate observed that the whites seemed to feel they were in an enemy's country that was 'in a state of war'.[27] The Commissioner of Crown Lands on the Darling Downs reflected that in the early 1840s the Aborigines were at 'open war with the Squatters'.[28] A settler wrote to the Sydney paper the *Colonist* in 1839 remarking:

> Now with reference to this colony, it is our opinion that the hostile and predatory tribes of Blacks can only be regarded in one of two lights; either as subjects in a state of armed and active rebellion, or as enemies arrayed in arms and waging war against Europeans as their invaders. It is absurd to talk of them merely in the light of occasional rioters; the history and character of their proceedings do not admit of any such construction.[29]

For years in some places, the Europeans on the frontier lived in a state of acute anxiety, never knowing where the Aborigines were. Shepherds and stockmen were speared, sheep and cattle were killed and stolen, and huts were robbed and burnt to the ground. As far as the frontiersmen were concerned, it was

> sheer nonsense to talk of apprehending them. You must either shoot a few of them by way of example or you must abandon the country altogether.[30]

So were the frontier settlers locked into inescapable conflict, always latent in the colonial situation? Was it bound to recur every time they took up new country and forced themselves on the resident clans? And if they were fighting a kind of war over the control of land and water, was their violence excessive? Did it go beyond what was necessary to achieve their ends?

Given the scattered nature of frontier conflict, these are questions that cannot easily be answered. There was no central direction or control of the conflict, no policy-making body, no overall strategy, no chain of command. Every squatter — and sometimes every group of neighbouring squatters — had to decide in isolation how to deal with the local clans; how much violence was required and when the Aborigines could be let in to live on the station. It is virtually impossible to decide if there was a general intention to destroy hostile Aboriginal groups or whether violence was used with the end of achieving dominance over, rather than exterminating, the tribes in question.

Undoubtedly there were times when parties of Europeans — squatters and workers alike — came together and went out into the bush with the intention of indiscriminately attacking the local clans. Such organised expeditions usually followed long periods of low-scale conflict or instances when Europeans had been attacked and killed. Revenge expeditions of this sort often resulted in considerable loss of life and the intention may sometimes have been to wipe out the group thought guilty of the offence.

An early settler on the New England Tableland wrote an account of one such punitive expedition carried out in 1841 following an attack on an outstation that had resulted in the death of three shepherds and the running-off of a flock of 2000 sheep. With two neighbouring squatters and seven workers, the party was brought together ready for revenge. All the station workers were 'savagely anxious and eager to be chosen for this painfully imperative task'. The thought of their butchered comrades 'made them pant for an opportunity of vengeance'. Eventually the party tracked the Aborigines to a camp site and shot into the group from two sides. 'Shot after shot, with curses wild and deep, the excited fellows launched at their hated foes'. Their murdered comrades were that night 'fearfully avenged'.[31]

During the 1830s and 1840s senior Colonial Office officials believed that the frontier settlers in New South Wales were exterminating the Aborigines. James Stephen clearly thought that violence was the main cause of death. The only solution he could think of was to arm the Aborigines and teach them to fight back. In Sydney, Governor Gipps spoke of justice and humanity but knew his appeal would not be heard out on the troubled, distant frontiers. Some settlers talked openly of extermination and perhaps a majority thought that such an outcome, if not necessarily desirable, was probably inevitable. Much of the violence was small-scale skirmishing between groups of frontiersmen and resident clans. It was often personal, immediate and spontaneous. When larger parties were organised to sweep across whole districts for days or even weeks on end, we find situations which do approximate with what the contemporary literature defines as genocidal massacres. How common they were is open to conjecture.

This question will be considered further when we look at the situation of Queensland between 1859 and 1897.

SEVEN

DISPERSING THE BLACKS

WITH THE DECISION in 1850 to grant the colonies of eastern Australia self-government, the Colonial Office prepared to surrender responsibility for the Aborigines to the very colonists whom they had frequently accused of trying to exterminate the tribes they encountered.

The problem had been apparent in the late 1840s, when the imperial government was deciding what to do about Aboriginal rights on land to which the squatters had been given leasehold title. The Colonial Office's suspicion of the colonists resurfaced. In a memo to his officials in 1847, the secretary of state, Earl Grey, remarked that it was essential to provide for continued Aboriginal access to pastoral land 'with a view to their preservation from being exterminated'.[1] He also sought to point out to the colonists the obligations they owed the Aborigines, for

> In assuming their Territory the settlers in Australia have incurred a moral obligation of the most sacred kind to make all necessary provision for the instruction and improvement of the Natives.[2]

The sense of moral obligation was stronger in London than in the antipodes, more persuasive in the minds of colonial governors than in those of members of the new Australian ministries. And there was certainly less concern about the fate of the Aborigines in Brisbane than in Sydney.

But there seemed to be little public concern when responsibility for all the Aborigines north of the Tweed River passed from London to Sydney in 1856 and then from Sydney to Brisbane three years later. Each step took responsibility closer to the frontier and placed it more securely in the hands of men with both public and private interests in the pastoral industry and in the rapid sale of land throughout the vast tropical hinterland.

Pastoral settlement in Queensland had begun in 1840, the pioneer squatters coming north from the troubled and often violent frontier in the broad river-valleys of northern New South Wales. The first parties rode up onto the Darling Downs heavily armed, expecting trouble. The Leslie brothers, for example, took 'plenty of firearms for fear of the blacks' on their expedition north. George Leslie wrote to his parents explaining that the party intended

> to build our huts in a square and have all the windows looking into the square and have the outside walls double slabbed [with] portholes and if we find the blacks disagreeable we will get a ten pounder and I expect that will astonish them.[3]

Apparently the brothers did not actually build a fort on their station at Canning Downs, but they did adopt highly aggressive policies towards the resident Aborigines. George Leslie wrote:

> We never allow them to come about the station or hold any communication with them except it be with a gun or sword.[4]

Reflecting on his experience as a Downs pioneer, C. P. Hodgson remarked that the earliest inroads of the settlers were 'marked with blood, the forests were ruthlessly seized, and the native tenants hunted down like their native dogs'.[5]

The new Queensland government inherited the Native Police Force, which had first entered what was to become the new colony in May 1849. After a period of disorganisation in the mid-1850s, the force was assured of future support by two well-planned, large-scale Aboriginal attacks on frontier stations: on the Fraser family at *Hornet Bank* in 1857 and on the Wills family and their employees at *Cullin-la-ringoe* in 1861, when nineteen Europeans were killed. Two parliamentary committees came out in favour of the force: a New South Wales select committee in 1858 and a Queensland one in 1861.

In his 1858 report, committee chairman Arthur Hodgson remarked that while the members repudiated, in the strongest terms, 'any attempt to wage a war of extermination against the Aborigines', they were satisfied that there was no alternative but to 'carry through matters with a strong hand, and punish with necessary severity all future outrages upon life and property'.[6] Following the killing of the Frasers, the duties of the Native Police officers were set down by the commandant, E. V. Morisset. They were to use every exertion to prevent the Aboriginal troopers from having 'any communication whatever' with tribes resident in districts where the detachment was stationed or was travelling through. Contact was to be of an entirely different kind, as the tenth and final instruction indicated:

It is the duty of the officers at all times and opportunities to disperse any large assemblage of blacks; such meetings, if not prevented, invariably lead to depredations or murder; and nothing but the mistaken kindness of the Officers in command inspired the blacks with sufficient confidence to commit the late fearful outrages on the Dawson Rivers. The Officers will therefore see the necessity of teaching the aborigines that no outrage or depredation shall be committed with impunity — but on the contrary, retributive justice shall speedily follow the Commission of crime; nevertheless the Officers will be careful in receiving reports against the blacks, as it frequently happens that mistakes are made to the identity of the aggressors. In the case of any collision with aborigines a report is to be forwarded to the Commandant without delay.[7]

These instructions remained the only written outline of the official duties of the Native Police and were not rescinded until 1896. Given their importance in understanding the aims and attitudes of successive Queensland administrations – and assessing whether there ever was genocidal intent – it is necessary to examine their implementation in some detail.

Very few records of the Native Police have survived, but we are allowed a glimpse of the activities of one detachment, under Lieutenant Wheeler, just after the separation of Queensland from New South Wales. Wheeler was questioned about an incident by the Queensland select committee of 1861. The exchange included these questions and answers:

Do those troopers understand English sufficiently to comprehend your orders? *Oh, yes.*

Did you give them orders to go into the scrub? *Yes.*

What was the nature of those orders? *I told them to surround the camp of Telemon blacks, and to disperse them.*

What do you mean by dispersing? *Firing at them. I give strict orders not to shoot any gins. It is only sometimes, when it is dark, that a gin is mistaken for a black-fellow, or might be wounded inadvertently.*

Do you think it is a proper thing to fire upon the blacks in that way? *If they are the right mob, of which I have every certainty.*

I can understand this – if there are warrants out against certain men, and they take to the scrub, that your troopers are ordered to follow them, and, if they do not stop when called upon in the Queen's name, to fire upon them, but in this case there were no warrants out. I wish to know what induced you to give those orders? *The letters I had received from several squatters, complaining that the blacks were robbing their huts, threatening their lives and spearing their cattle and sheep.*[8]

Numerous points can be made with reference to Morisset's instructions and Wheeler's evidence. Enormous power and discretion had been handed to the Native Police officers — literally, power over life and death. They could decide how big a 'large gathering' had to be before it qualified for dispersal, and what constituted a depredation. Was it one hut robbed, one cow speared? They could decide which was the guilty mob and how many of them should be shot. On the frontier they became investigating officers, magistrates, judge, jury and executioner. As Wheeler indicated, by the late 1850s all pretence of following up and executing warrants had been dispensed with. Without Colonial Office supervision, such legal niceties were quickly cast aside.

The report of the select committee on the Native Police was accepted in the parliament with only the one dissenting voice, that of Dr Henry Challinor, an Ipswich magistrate who had endeavoured without success to take action against Lieutenant Wheeler. His stand against indiscriminate violence won him few friends. His parliamentary colleagues spoke openly of the need to use violence against the blacks, both in the debate that resulted in setting up the select committee and in the one that approved the report. Radcliffe Pring, the attorney-general, left no doubt in anyone's mind what the term 'disperse' in the commandant's instructions referred to. It was, he said, 'idle to dispute' that it meant 'nothing but firing into them' in order to deal out retributive justice 'when it was deserved'.[9]

His colleagues talked openly of war. John Watts observed that the people of Queensland 'must be considered to be, as they always had been, at open war with the Aborigines'.[10] In the second debate he declared that the settlers must 'hold the land by force or not at all'. The blacks had to be regarded in the same light as inhabitants of a country under martial law and they 'must be taught to feel the mastery of the whites', which could only be achieved by the Aborigines' fear of the carbine. There was no other way of ruling them and the carbine must be resorted to.[11]

Mr Gore agreed that the whites and blacks were in a state of war and that it was necessary to establish 'the superiority of the white race by means of military force'.[12] A number of members believed the Aborigines would inevitably disappear, because it had always been found that 'an inferior barbarous race disappeared before a superior and civilized one.'[13] The colonial Treasurer agreed, declaring that:

> We should be sorry to see the natives treated with cruelty or oppression; but that the settlers will increase, and the colony expand, is a result which the rules of nature render positively certain. We could not, if we would, interfere with the event; and if the inferior race suffers in the process, that is only what has happened in all such cases, and will happen again to the end of time.[14]

While numerous speakers skirted around the question of the total destruction of the Aborigines, a prominent solicitor and future premier (1866, 1866–67, 1874–76), Arthur Macalister, openly declared:

> If extermination were desired – and that appeared to be all that could be done – then the black police were the only force that could be employed.[15]

Criticism of the force and doubts about its legality were overwhelmed by the public outrage that resulted from the Aboriginal attack on *Cullin-la-ringoe* station in November 1861. As a correspondent writing to the *North Australian* observed:

> now we can understand and can appreciate the value of that much abused force . . . we thank Providence for it, and commend it to its work.[16]

For the next twenty years the troopers patrolled the frontier dispersing and dealing out 'retributive justice'. Governments of all persuasions brushed criticism aside, although they were occasionally forced to initiate inquiries into alleged atrocities. Police numbers fluctuated, rising from

128 in 1861 to 200 in the early 1870s, where they remained until the early 1880s. Although it was a much cheaper force than any possible alternative, Queensland spent the not inconsiderable sum of £318 000 on it during the 1860s and 1870s.

Not until 1880 was there a serious public re-examination of the purpose and function of the force. An intense campaign for a royal commission launched by the weekly paper the *Queenslander* sparked two long debates in the parliament during which government and opposition members declared their views on their frontier force. In detailing the force's brutal work, the *Queenslander* used harsh, uncompromising language:

> Of this force we have already said that it is impossible to write about it with patience. It is enough to say of it that this body, organised and paid for by us, is sent to do work which its officers are forbidden to report in detail, and that a true record would shame us before our fellow countrymen in every part of the British Empire.
>
> When the police have entered on the scene, then the conflict goes on apace. It is a fitful war of extermination waged upon the blacks, something after the fashion in which other settlers wage war upon noxious wild beasts, the process differing only in so far as the victims, being human, are capable of a wider variety of suffering than brutes. The savages, hunted from their places where they have been accustomed to find food, driven into barren ranges, shot like wild dogs at sight, when and how they can.[17]

It was confronting journalism, but did the members of parliament consider that they were promoting 'a fitful war of extermination' around the ragged frontiers of settlement and had been so doing for the previous twenty years? Perhaps they didn't, but grudgingly or not, they agreed with the *Queenslander*'s assertion that the term 'dispersal' was well understood and had been adopted into bush slang as a 'convenient euphemism for wholesale massacre'.[18]

The leading parliamentary critic of the force was John Douglas, who told his colleagues that at the present time the troopers

> did nothing else but shoot them down whenever they could get at them. That was the sole function of the native police. As far as could be judged from their instructions and practice, they were chiefly kept as a military force dispersing natives when they congregated, and patrolling districts to drive the blacks into positions where they would not come into contact with the European settlers.[19]

Though speaking from the Opposition benches, Douglas had been in the parliament since 1863, a cabinet minister between 1866 and 1869 and premier from March 1877 to January 1879. He also held the portfolio of Colonial Secretary from 7 November 1877 to 21 January 1879 and therefore had ministerial responsibility for the Native Police for fourteen months. When he denounced the force in parliament in October 1880 his views carried the weight of recent ministerial experience and knowledge of the records. He probably knew much more than he felt able to divulge in public.

Opposing Douglas in the House was the present colonial secretary, A.H. Palmer, another experienced politician and frontier squatter. Palmer asserted that the frontier settlers invented stories about massacres and that the best liars were the Native Police officers. After listening to them for half an hour, he said, one would almost wonder that there was a black-fellow left in the colony.[20] Palmer also insisted that the Native Police were not instructed to disperse the blacks but merely to patrol their districts, and

> as far as they could, to get into communication with the blacks and try and make them understand as far as possible what we often hear in child's play: 'If you let me alone I will let you alone'.[21]

The image of relatively benign exchange slipped later in the speech, with Palmer fulminating that the nature of the blacks was 'so treacherous that they were only guided by fear', that in fact it was only possible to rule 'a savage race, and the Australian aboriginal in particular' by brute force and by showing him 'that you are his master'.[22] In private, Palmer was in agreement with Douglas about Native Police practices. In a letter written to the distinguished ethnographer A. W. Howitt two years after the debate on the question, Palmer declared that he sympathised with 'the unfortunate blacks the way they are treated'. They had no place to go and 'wherever they are seen by the Native Police, the rule has been to shoot them'. Palmer had been the minister responsible for the force from 1879 to 1881.[23]

The description of the activities of the Native Police by Douglas in public and Palmer in private matched exactly what the attorney-general had said in 1861. The force dispersed groups of Aborigines by firing into them. The explanation that the police took action while endeavouring to arrest known offenders was no longer even mentioned. Retributive justice had become an accepted fact of frontier life and eventually the force dealt out death indiscriminately to ease the path of the pioneer. The violence had become pre-emptive. In the process, large numbers of Aborigines were killed. No-one had any doubt about that; the public debate was not *if* Aborigines were shot down but whether such killing was necessary and justifiable.

Members of parliament made the most casual, passing references to the number of blacks who had been killed. While debating supply for the Native Police in 1880, prominent politician and former premier (1876–77) George Thorn argued that the force was only required in the coastal districts, because elsewhere the blacks were 'pretty well shot down and got rid of'. On the Warrego he had not seen any Aborigines at all and was told they had 'all been shot down by the police'. He believed the 'same thing was going on in the west of Rockhampton' presently.[24] John Douglas remarked in the same debate that:

> Within the last year or two . . . brutalities and murders – deliberate and cold blooded murders, unjustified by any retaliating act – had been over and over again committed in the north . . .[25]

Douglas's colleague, Boyd Morehead, then a cabinet minister and future premier (1888–1890), had no doubt that the 'blacks had suffered great injustice' by being hunted down and shot, but in many cases they had 'got only what they thoroughly deserved'.[26]

Queensland newspapers carried frequent reports of dispersals, sometimes within the towns themselves or on their outskirts, along with accounts of dead bodies being left where they fell and of officers boasting of their exploits among the tribes. It would be possible to fill volumes with such press clippings, but a short selection will provide some idea of the public knowledge of the activities of the force.

A Rockhampton correspondent wrote to the Brisbane papers about this 'mismanaged and most disgraceful force'. The town itself had

> witnessed scenes in its neighbourhood which one hardly dare relate – the bloodiest of murders committed upon the innocent natives at one time, followed by the greatest solicitude upon the part of those who saw the deeds that they should not be talked about. It has witnessed a drunken officer, too beastly almost to sit upon his horse, ride forth, with the avowed and inflamed intention of 'shooting down the wretches'.[27]

A few days later a Brisbane correspondent observed:

> As one murder after another of the aboriginals of Queensland is recorded in your paper, and we hear no denial of the report, nor any investigation into the circumstances attending the wholesale slaughter of those who are debarred from English laws, of which they are ignorant – and from our courts of justice, where their evidence will not be taken – we really become heart sick.
>
> It is not enough that we occupy what was their country, and leave them to the horrors of unmitigated starvation, but a number of paid ruffians, led on by white fellows . . . shoot down the unoffending and the useful of them – like dogs, while the innocent blood thus shed lies at the door of our Executive Council.[28]

In 1876 the editor of the *Brisbane Courier* expressed concern about the absolute discretion left in the hands of the Native Police officers and that some of them had carried out their duties with 'an unnatural ferocity'. It was with them 'a war of extermination'.[29] A colleague at the far end of the colony had similar thoughts, which he expressed in an editorial in the *Cooktown Courier*:

> Putting it in plain English this is what we Queenslanders do. When we come into a new district, we bring with us the Native Police, a body of trained savages armed for the destruction of their countrymen. We never make any attempt to soothe the suspicions or maintain friendly relations with the aboriginal inhabitants of the soil, but we set the Native Police on them to make them 'quiet'. This is effected by the trained savages surprising their countrymen whenever an occasion offers, and massacring them indiscriminately.[30]

Running parallel with the conflict between the Native Police and the Aboriginal tribes was a private campaign waged by the settlers themselves. Sometimes they called in the Native Police to punish local clans, but they often took revenge themselves, particularly if the force was out of the district. There were numerous, if often veiled, references to private punitive expeditions in many colonial newspapers. For much of the time in the 1860s and 1870s the squatters determined to 'keep them out' or drive the Aborigines off their runs whenever they were seen. A correspondent writing to the *Port Denison Times* explained that 'keeping them out' involved:

> never to allow them near a camp, outstation, head station or township; consequently they were hunted by anyone if seen in open country, and driven away or shot down when caught out of the scrub and broken ground.[31]

If much of the killing lay at the door of the executive council, how did the members of the Queensland parliament explain and justify their actions? They clearly rejected the idea firmly established by the Colonial Office in the 1830s that the Aborigines were British subjects who were within the Queen's peace; that it was a grave error 'to regard them as Aliens with whom a war can exist'. [32]

Such a view was openly contested in debates in the first years of self-government. Gore, a Darling Downs pioneer, told his parliamentary colleagues in 1861 that the problem of what to do about Aborigines was surrounded by false assumptions, one of which was that the blacks were British subjects and were 'amenable to and entitled to the protection of the law the same as white people'. This, he declared, was false. [33] In 1880 Henry King said much the same thing, arguing that

> all the evils of the present system arose out of the injustice of the law in this respect — that the law assumed the blacks to be British subjects, and consequently they could not be punished until after trial, whilst in point of fact they were not British subjects but their enemies. [34]

Given the widespread acceptance of the idea that the Aborigines were enemies rather than subjects in rebellion, the technically illegal actions of the Native Police and private vigilante parties were widely accepted as a realistic response to local conditions. A Native Police officer spoke in confidence to a reporter from the *Sydney Morning Herald* in 1880 and in explanation — or exculpation — of a recent atrocity said that the blacks were not like ordinary criminals:

> They would not be arrested. Not one of them would ever be brought in alive, so that there was nothing for it but to take their lives. If they were left to pursue their depredations, the white settlers may as well leave the country, and if they were to be pursued there was no other course but to kill them. [35]

The editor of the *Brisbane Courier* discussed the same issues in a leader of April 1876. Throughout the far north and the north-western districts, he observed, there can be no doubt that we still hold possession by virtue of a kind of conquest. If the aborigines were more civilized than they are, we should either make treaties with them, or we should be at open war with them. It would then be either peace or war on certain terms, and we should be guided by the principles of action recognized in such cases. But the scattered tribes of Australian natives . . . have to be dealt with in detail, and the process is a very undefined one, certainly not strictly justified under the civil law; and yet the exigencies of the case are not sufficiently urgent to demand the application of martial law.[36]

By the 1880s there was a widespread view that conflict was an inevitable consequence of colonisation. A correspondent writing to the *Queenslander* in 1880 admitted that the blacks were treated with 'gross injustice', but that the primary and fundamental injustice was the taking of their country and if settlement was to proceed then a certain amount of cruelty and severity was justified.[37] In similar vein another correspondent asked the critical questions, 'What lives are we to sacrifice — black or white? Are we to protect the black or protect the white?' In parliament, Lumley Hill observed that

it must not be forgotten that the white man had undertaken to settle the country, to occupy it, and bring it as it were, into civilization, and the blacks must always be a secondary consideration to him. The blacks must give way to the whites, and recede beyond the bounds of civilization.[38]

Constant reference to warfare and the necessity to defeat the Aboriginal tribes in order to facilitate the progress of settlement led many contemporaries to see their situation as comparable with other colonists who were engaged in war. In 1879 the editor of the *Queenslander* remarked that 'we are today at open war with every tribe of wild blacks on the frontier of settlement'.[39] His colleague at the *Rockhampton Bulletin* similarly observed that there was:

no way of treating them, except as belligerents when they commit outrages, has yet been found efficacious in the back tracks. They may be tolerated and treated kindly so long as they refrain from mischievous acts, but when they rob, steal or murder, they must be treated as enemies of state and shot down with as little compunction as soldiers shoot each other in battles amongst civilized man.[40]

The settlers' points of reference changed with the years. At the time of separation from New South Wales in 1859, comparison was made with the Indian Mutiny. The *Moreton Bay Courier* asserted that the Aborigines had claimed more victims than the massacre at Cawnpore,[41] while a correspondent observed that the number of murders in central Queensland was 'greater in ratio to the Killings in the Mutiny'.[42] In the 1860s the colonists compared their situation with that of New Zealand, while twenty years later they referred to events in the Sudan and Zululand. Expenditure on defence was compared with what was spent on the 'repression of the enemy within our gates'.[43] A north Queensland selector wrote to the *Queenslander* in 1887, observing that

there are thousands, that can be spent on Defence Forces, to protect the inhabitants of this country from the invisible, perhaps imaginary, but for certain distant enemies; but we cannot afford to keep an efficient body of police to keep in check the enemies we have at our door, the enemy of every day, the one who slowly but surely robs us and impoverishes us.[44]

Queensland colonists sought to crush all Aboriginal resistance to the rapid expansion of settlement. Many of them saw this as an inescapable consequence of colonisation. But did they seek to go beyond that and 'get rid of' the Aborigines altogether? Was there a genocidal impulse in the behaviour and aspirations of the Queenslanders?

The question of extermination was openly discussed in Queensland in the same way it was in Tasmania in the 1820s and in New South Wales in the 1830s and 1840s, although by the 1880s the conviction that the Aborigines were a dying race was even more firmly fixed in the popular mind. Norwegian scientist Carl Lumholtz, who spent several years in Queensland in the 1880s, observed that while in the colony he had often heard it 'openly avowed' that the country would never be what it ought until the blacks were exterminated.[45] The Rev. Tennyson Woods was told by a senior government official that while it was all very well to have sympathy with the blacks, the colony 'could not get on until they were exterminated'.[46] Such sentiments were expressed in the press, too, a correspondent writing to the *Queenslander* in 1880 arguing that if the Native Police was an exterminating force the pity was that the work was not more effectually done. 'Is there room for both of us here?' he asked rhetorically, and answered that there was not and that 'the sooner the weaker is wiped out the better'.[47]

The editor of the *Cooktown Courier*, Carl Feilberg, believed that the whole question of Aboriginal policy could be summed up in two questions:

> Do we intend to exterminate the blacks, or keep them quiet? The former result we have not the means of achieving; the second will never be attained by our present fitful scheme of haphazard little massacres.

The authorities, he argued, should make up their minds as to what course they intended to pursue:

> If they intend to attempt the extermination of the race, then the system of haphazard shooting might become intelligible. But they would have to face this difficulty. The armed force of native police would have to be ten times as numerous as at present, they would have to go over the district in the same manner as sportsmen in the old country go over a hunting field; they would drive the savage to absolute desperation and perhaps cause a loss of many European lives, and judging from the history of Tasmania, they would probably find in the long run that the task could not be thoroughly accomplished.[48]

Feilberg was an acute observer of colonial society. His rhetorical question as to the intention of the government was an understandable one. Two years earlier, the member for the far northern Queensland electorate of Kennedy, J. M. Macrossan, had made a similar observation to his parliamentary colleagues, referring to the system of continual warfare that was 'being carried out at present to utter extermination'.[49]

Queensland governments were clearly aware of what the Native Police did; they approved and paid for the force and rejected criticism of the bloody work of dispersal. But its activities were never publicised or even discussed very often, and so much discretion was placed in the hands of the commandant – and even more in those of individual officers – that it is difficult to know how ministerial responsibility was exercised. From their speeches it is clear that Queensland politicians accepted the necessity for retributive and pre-emptive violence, to punish those who had made attacks on the settlers or their property or who might do so in the future.

Protecting the pioneer became a colonial obsession. The editor of the *North Australian* wrote:

> So injurious to the best interests of the colony do the outrages by the blacks become, in deterring settlement and keeping out capital, that we look upon them as the worst evil of our position, and as the greatest barrier to the development of our resources.[50]

Mr Watts, the Darling Downs pioneer, told parliament that it was 'absolutely necessary to protect the settler in his forward march'.[51] The editor of the *Queensland Guardian* was in agreement, observing that the settlers had decided 'beyond dispute' that they would occupy the land and that 'all opposition must be overcome'.[52]

Attacks on Aboriginal society were instrumental rather than ideological. The overriding objective was occupation and development of the land. If that could be done without bloodshed, well and good, but if the blacks resisted they had to be crushed. If extermination was required many colonists were willing to countenance it — although others were appalled at the prospect. The *Moreton Bay Courier* saw the alternative in stark terms, to choose either 'an exterminating warfare against them, or to abandon our outstations'.[53] It was a view reiterated eight years later out on the frontier in central Queensland, the editor of the *Peak Downs Telegram* declaring:

> a war of extermination is the only policy to pursue, the alternative being an abandonment of the country which no sane man will advocate for an instant.[54]

Such extreme violence could be considered because of the strength of racist sentiment, the contempt for Aboriginal society as a whole. Perhaps the most brutal and callous comment was made by a correspondent to the *Queenslander* who declared: 'And being a useless race, what does it matter what they suffer'.[55]

A month later another correspondent was a little more expansive if no more compassionate. 'North Gregory' explained that:

> If the whites are to settle and occupy their country, then a certain amount of cruelty and severity is unavoidable. You say we treat them like wild animals. Well, to a certain extent their attributes are the same, and must be met in the same manner.[56]

Feilberg's uncertainty about whether the government intended to exterminate the Aborigines was a reasonable response to the evidence available to him. Even with the Native Police at its full strength of over 200 troopers, it could do little more than disperse the groups it actually 'dropped across' and move on. This pre-emptive violence was as much an indication of the inadequacy of the paramilitary forces available to the government as of their strength. A sharp reprisal, a pre-emptive dispersal, might, it was hoped, keep the blacks intimidated until the police could return, perhaps months into the future.

The frenetic demands of the frontier settlers for protection arose from the small and scattered nature of European settlement and their vulnerability to Aboriginal hostility. Once a district was thought to be pacified the Native Police moved on, regardless of how many Aborigines had survived the killing times.

At the other end of the spectrum of contact, the police did not even venture into those remote and inhospitable districts that had no attraction for the settler. At any one time dispersals were confined to a comparatively narrow band of territory on the outskirts of European occupation. Having crushed all overt opposition, there was no particular passion to continue the business of murder – certainly not enough to spend time and public money on the process. Until the turn of the nineteenth century, Queensland governments had little interest in the Aborigines once they ceased to threaten life, property and progress.

Perhaps more to the point was the widespread assumption that the Aborigines were destined to die out anyway, regardless of human agency. This view was apparent from the initial creation of the colony in 1859, with the editor of the *Moreton Bay Courier* remarking in February of that year that the race may be dying out and that if there was not in that fact a solution to the problem of their hostility, 'we might write in strong language that it was time the whole race was exterminated'.[57] In 1867 the editor of the *Rockhampton Bulletin* wrote of his opposition to much of the violence used against the Aborigines because it was both unnecessary and superfluous, and because

> whilst we regard the disappearance of the black race before the face of the white man as an inevitable fact to which we must of necessity submit as one of the conditions of successful colonisation, we must protest in the name of humanity and justice against seeking to attain this end by a ruthless and indiscriminate extermination of the doomed race. Their extinction is only a matter of time, and no unnecessary cruelty should be used to effect a result which the operation of natural causes will certainly accomplish.[58]

There is no doubt that many frontier settlers were glad when the local Aborigines were 'let in' to township and station. They became an indispensable source of cheap labour and available sex in a highly masculine society. The editor of the *Queensland Guardian* wrote in 1861 that he hoped that

> it will prove of these lowest of mankind that the necessity for hunting them down like wild beasts will cease, and that they will escape extermination by becoming worthy to live.[59]

As cheap labourers, and casual sexual partners, the Aborigines found sanctuary of a sort on the fringes of white society. Many had escaped extermination, if not the poverty, disease and malnutrition that followed in the wake of the killing times, and they may have been more destructive in the long run of both life and well-being.

Was Queensland guilty of genocide? There is certainly much evidence available for retrospective prosecution. There was great loss of life and frequent talk of extermination, both within the parliament and beyond it. Serious scholars have passed sentence on the colony, but the prosecution has a number of difficulties to contend with. When the killing was done by the settlers themselves, we know comparatively little of their intent beyond the few dozen or so individuals who recorded their actions and motivation. Reticence in such cases was to be expected. We are dealing with hundreds of individuals in many parts of a large colony over a period of fifty years. Motives probably varied widely according to time, place, local circumstances and personality. Punitive expeditions probably brought together disparate people who agreed only on the need for immediate action and who were then forever linked by haunting memories of carnage. Violence no doubt sprang up out of particular local events and spiralled uncontrollably towards reciprocal vendetta.

What of the Native Police? We are hampered by the loss or

destruction of records, but enough is known to frame a general indictment. Were all governments that financed and directed the force from 1859 to 1896, and thereby sanctioned dispersals, guilty of genocide? If interrogated on the question, Queensland ministers of the time would no doubt have answered that Aborigines were killed in the course of a kind of warfare and because they threatened European life and property, and that what they wanted was indigenous acquiescence, not their disappearance.

And that takes our investigation back to one of the fundamental problems of genocidal scholarship, whether it relates to the past or the present. How do we distinguish between killing in warfare and killing conducted with intent to destroy a human group? Maybe the problem would be easier to solve if we altered our focus and looked more closely at events at a particular time and in a specific locality.

EIGHT

SUDDEN AND TERRIBLE RETRIBUTION: GENOCIDAL MOMENTS IN COLONIAL AUSTRALIA

GENOCIDE, AS WE HAVE SEEN, is a very specific crime: the intent to destroy, in whole or in part, a national, ethnical, racial or religious group. At first glance there would appear to be no problem in assessing whether this definition has any relevance to Australian history, however the matter might finally be judged. Aborigines could be construed as belonging to each, or all, of the four defined categories – national, ethnical, racial or religious.

But should we deal with Aboriginal society all over the continent as the group to be considered – or those groups that happened to live within the various colonial boundaries drawn up in Downing Street, half a world away? Each option has something going for it. There were broad social and cultural uniformities across the continent. Despite very real differences, Aborigines were all more like each other than they were like any other cultural group beyond the continent. If genocide is pre-eminently a crime of state, the colonial boundaries delineated the limits of authority and the compass of legal and moral responsibility. And if the settlers and their governments defined the diverse indigenous societies as all being 'Queensland Blacks', is that where our investigation should rest? Modern genocide scholarship has emphasised the importance of group definition by the perpetrator and that principle would certainly simplify our investigation. But it would also distort it.

Should we consider the problem of which groups are to be examined anthropologically – or from an Aboriginal perspective? The idea of there being a category called the 'Queensland Blacks' would have been meaningless to Aborigines living within the colonial boundaries. To proceed further, we have to face the difficulty of bringing to bear a precise legal definition as enshrined in an international convention onto the complex and shifting patterns of Aboriginal social and political organisation. If we are to replace the European category 'Aboriginal' or 'Queensland Black' with a more anthropologically refined one, which should we choose? Should our unit of concern be the tribe or nation – that is, the large but often loose coalition of groups who intermarried and were united by language (or at least dialect) and cultural traditions? This would make a lot of sense, but such large groups rarely ever met at one time and could only do so when there was enough food and water to facilitate a coming-together. Should we therefore be dealing with the small local groups in which most Aborigines spent much of their time? After all, it may well have been local groups that characteristically made the decisions to attack the settlers who had usurped their particular range.

The paradox is that the smaller the group to be considered, the greater the likelihood that genocide did actually take place, that many – and sometimes most – members of local groups were killed by settlers or by Aboriginal troopers or trackers and that there was an intention to do so. Considered in this way, genocide would be judged to be more common but less momentous, in that the numbers involved in each incident would be quite small and the perpetrators may have had no idea that their local adversaries represented a distinct group.

This brings us to the question of what in the literature have been called genocidal massacres – the episodic killing of particular members of a group that still falls short of genocide proper. The distinction depends very much on what size of group we are talking about. A massacre involving, say, thirty or forty victims may be of relative unimportance if considered as one incident in the continent-wide history of Aboriginal Australia – or even Aboriginal Queensland. But the picture would change dramatically if viewed from the other end of the spectrum, from the perspective of the tribe or the local group. The killing of that many people might literally have meant its destruction and disappearance, even if some members survived physically. The refugees, as a result of the massacre, may have been driven out of their country, or they may not have been in a position to sustain their group life, maintain cultural traditions or bestow or receive appropriate marriage partners. And the death toll would also represent an irreplaceable loss of knowledge, skills and stories that were dependent on memory and oral tradition. Killing people in such circumstances would be analogous to burning books and destroying manuscripts, images and shrines.

At this point it would be appropriate to consider a number of case studies of events confined in time and space – of attacks by settlers and police on particular Aboriginal groups in the second half of the nineteenth century. The studies relate to the Dawson River basin in central Queensland, the Channel Country in far south-western Queensland, the region around Alice Springs and the west Kimberley in Western Australia.

In the late 1850s and early 1860s the European settlers faced strong Aboriginal resistance as they took up river frontages throughout the Fitzroy basin of central Queensland. The local Aborigines made repeated attacks on sheep and cattle and frequently speared isolated shepherds. Arthur Hodgson, a pioneer squatter and politician, told his colleagues in the New South Wales parliament in June 1858 that there had been thirty whites killed on the Dawson in the previous twelve months.[1] Uppermost in the minds of colonial society was the attack on *Hornet Bank* station on 27 October 1857, during which a party of the local Jiman men killed eleven Europeans, including the widow, Mrs Fraser, seven of her nine children and three employees. Mrs Fraser and two of her daughters were raped before death. An even larger massacre occurred in October 1861 to the north of *Hornet Bank* at *Cullin-la-ringoe* station on the Nagoa River, where nineteen men, women and children were killed by the local Wadja people. Horatio Wills, the lessee of the station, was a well-known and respected figure in colonial Australia who was considered to have been friendly towards the blacks. Both massacres had elements which horrified and enraged public opinion; both called forth savage and massive reprisals. The intense anger of the time was important in explaining the colonists' behaviour, their *dolus specialis* that facilitated and justified massacre.

Responding to the first news of *Hornet Bank*, the editor of the *North Australian* denounced the 'ruthless savages, whose appetite for blood seems to increase in proportion to the number of victims'. They were 'detestable monsters . . . a race of beings totally destitute of the common attributes of humanity', who should be dealt with accordingly.[2] The *Moreton Bay Free Press* referred to the 'ruthless savages' who threatened the progress of civilisation on the frontier and whose 'bloodthirsty spirit' endangered the lives of all pioneers. Retribution must be exacted, but to be effective it had to 'fall upon them suddenly and terribly'. In fact, their absence from the earth would be 'rather a blessing than a curse'.[3] Opinion in the hinterland was probably even more inflamed, the Gayndah correspondent of the *Moreton Bay Courier* writing in anger:

> if it is wrong to hold the country – give it up; if it is right – hold it as of old, peaceably if possible but when such terrible proof is given of the impossibility of peace, treat them as they deserve; [if] it is useless trying to tame them, then destroy them, as you would any other savage beast, men they do not deserve to be called.[4]

The spirited resistance on the Dawson appeared to be a direct challenge to the whole colonising venture. The editor of the *North Australian* called for reprisals that would be the only way to ensure the security of the squatters and insisted that if action was not effective one of the finest grazing districts in the colony would 'have to be vacated and left to the original inhabitants who have no right to occupy the soil'.[5] No-one, it seems, called publicly for the normal application of the law — for investigation, arrest and trial. Indeed, the attempt to 'carry out English law in the case of the black' was a 'manifest absurdity'.[6] A correspondent writing from the Burnett district observed that the experience of life on the frontier had always shown that the law was 'nearly powerless for the punishment of guilty savages' and as a result it was only natural to suppose that the settlers had to take the law into their own hands.[7] Frederick Sinnett, a special correspondent for the Melbourne *Argus*, travelled through central Queensland in the aftermath of *Hornet Bank* and found that the relations between the 'black and white races' were a matter of 'war to the knife'. He reported the comments of a prominent settler 'enjoying great respect', who explained to Sinnett that

> if he fell in with a strange party of blacks in the bush he would ride straight at them with his revolver, and shoot right and left, and this is not in any vengeful or bloodthirsty spirit, but because the state of warfare between the races is so virulent that if he showed hesitation about attacking them, they would be sure to attack him, and thus it would become a mere point of tactics to strike the first blow.[8]

The public reaction three years later to the news of the killing at *Cullin-la-ringoe* was even more vociferous, with many people calling openly for the massacre of the whole tribe, for action 'as will strike terror into the murderous crew'.[9] The news of the deaths was so sudden and horrible 'as almost to take away all power of language or even thought'. The perpetrators were a 'treacherous and ruthless horde of savages — ruffians destitute of every trace of humanity — revelling in every kind of outrage, and battering on blood'.[10] At Taroom the greatest horror and indignation was felt by all classes in the district,[11] while in Rockhampton a 'universal cry of indignation burst forth'.[12] In the Burnett district the news of the Wills massacre 'cast a gloomy influence around' and all conversations related to it. 'Mercy and quarter' were the last things thought of.[13] Writing from *Orion Downs* station, the squatter Moore Dillon explained that when news of the massacre was received,

> an uncontrollable desire for vengeance took possession of every heart, words of execration and pity fell alike heedlessly upon the ear – the blood of strong men and helpless women, of grey-haired men and unconscious infants spilled wantonly on every side, spoke to every heart in a language words could not interpret.[14]

As was common in 1857, there were many public calls for large-scale, indiscriminate revenge. 'The tribe must be punished', a correspondent writing in the *Queensland Guardian* declared, 'whether it number scores or hundreds . . . the deadly bullet must do the work of the more legitimate executioner – justice must triumph over law'.[15]

Retribution fell suddenly and terribly on both the Jiman and the Wadja tribes and those whose country was in proximity to them along the Dawson, Comet and Nagoa rivers. In his study of *Hornet Bank, A Nest of Hornets*, Gordon Reid calculated that the Native Police and the settlers killed at least 150 Aborigines in a series of punitive expeditions extending over many weeks. The total death toll may have reached 300,[16] although it is impossible to arrive at a precise figure. For six weeks a party of squatters and their overseers, calling themselves 'the Browns', scoured the district seeking out and shooting anyone suspected of involvement in the attack on *Hornet Bank*. In his reminiscences of his part in the settlers' vendetta Ernest Davies observed that 'upon the whole they got their deserts at our hands, so far as it was within our power to deal out rough justice'.[17] George Lang, who visited central Queensland in the months after *Hornet Bank*, wrote in anguish to his uncle, John Dunmore Lang, about the ongoing vendetta:

> When I first arrived in the district the topic of general conversation was the murder of the Frazer family on the Dawson by the Blacks of that district and the hope was universally expressed that the atrocious actors in that

tragedy would meet with condign punishment. I joined in this hope believing in good faith that no illegal nor dishonourable not to say barbarous or inhuman means should be resorted to for that purpose. On my way to the interior however, I was undeceived as to the proposed method of punishing the Blacks and I now know that nothing could have been more unworthy of human beings than the procedure both of the members of the Police Force and the white population than their horrid indiscriminate murders of the Blacks.

I learned from various sources that a party of twelve — squatters and their confidential overseers — went out mounted and armed to the teeth and scoured the country for blacks, away from the scrubs of the murder of the Frazers altogether, and shot upwards of eighty men, women and children.[18]

Lang also reported that the Native Police claimed to have killed seventy people. Reid believed that Lang's estimate of 150 deaths must be taken as reliable and that it accorded with other evidence.[19]

The impact on the Jiman was catastrophic. Visitors to the Dawson in the months after the punitive expeditions had done their work observed the deep mourning apparent among the survivors. A party of Europeans who travelled for 140 kilometres along the river early in 1860 concluded that 'great destruction must have taken place among the tribe' which the people had not forgotten. A great part of every evening in the camps was taken up with singing what one of the Europeans called the beautiful, pathetic and melancholy lamentation for the dead. William Telfer, who was also in the district in 1860, reported that the howling of the blacks and their dogs kept his party awake all night. It was 'a most unearthly and weird dismal sound crying after their friends who had been shot by the native police'. Many of the survivors were wounded and

several of them had old gunshot wounds on their bodies some only quite young scarcely seventeen years old. Completely Crippled shot in the hips had to walk with two sticks as well as they Could it was a pitiful sight to see them trying to get along hopping about shot by the native police and others.[20]

It appears that the refugees from what Rosa Campbell Praed (whose father was a member of 'the Browns') called the 'little war' were scattered over a wide area of central Queensland, and by the twentieth century there were few traces left of their language and culture. Reid concluded in 1982 that there were no Jiman descendants. He referred to a national survey of Aboriginal communities conducted by the Department of Aboriginal Affairs in Canberra in 1979 that sought the names of tribes and tribal languages spoken, but failed to locate any members of the Jiman tribe. Commenting on their fate Reid observed:

> There may be individuals with Jiman blood, but it is unlikely that they are aware of it. Any who have such blood probably consider themselves to be Wakka Wakka [a neighbouring tribe]. The once strong people, who had been 'cock of the walk' on the Upper Dawson before the white settlers arrived, people with their own name, dialect, customs, traditions and land-identification, seem to have gone forever.[21]

The Wadja suffered a similar fate in the months after the attack on *Cullin-la-ringoe* as they were pursued by both the settlers and the Native Police, seven detachments of which were deployed in the region. In mid-December 1861 the *Rockhampton Bulletin* carried a report on the activities of the police, which was reprinted in many other newspapers in the colonies. It read:

> We are informed that on the 26th and 27th ultimo, the Native Police overtook the tribe of natives who committed the late outrage at Nagoa, and succeeded in driving them into a place from whence escape was impossible. They then shot down sixty or seventy, and then only ceased firing upon them when their ammunition was expended.[22]

In a dispatch to the Colonial Office in December, Governor Bowen explained that an estimated seventy Aborigines had been killed during the punitive raids of settlers and police. Despite the widespread publicity given to the death toll, there was never any official denial of the fact or amendment of the figures.[23]

The Queensland government was heavily criticised for both its direct involvement in the activities of the Native Police and its acquiescence in private vendettas. Perhaps the most eloquent and cogent condemnation was written by John West, the distinguished editor of the *Sydney Morning Herald*, in two editorials in early December 1861. West had some understanding of the immediate and violent response of the settlers, but the activities of the police force were another matter altogether. He wrote that although one might excuse the murderous volleys fired into the blacks' camps by the exasperated settlers, that was not the right mode of 'conducting our relations with the blacks under the sanction of the Government'. 'Is it a part of Her Majesty's domains?' he asked. Were these policemen paid by the Crown and furnished with arms and ammunition for such a service? West concluded that the only explanation that could be adduced for the 'wholesale destruction' was that the Queensland government had adopted a policy of extermination. He then asked the obvious question of whether extermination was an objective the government of a British colony ought to 'proclaim or assist'.[24] In his final assault on the policy of the northern colony, West concluded that there was an implicit policy to annihilate the race. 'We, of course,' he declared,

> know all the difficulties which environ these subjects, but we fear the evidence is irresistible that the destruction of the blacks is the aim as well as the result of our colonial policy: that we have undoubtedly acquiesced when we have not participated, and that the guilt of these horrible massacres must finally rest with the Government, which is too weak to prevent because it is unwilling to punish them. The butchery of those seventy people is a murder as cruel, cold blooded and inexcusable as any to be found in the annals of the race. We may excuse the settlers on account of the instant

provocation, when, according to their reports, some thirty perished, but the slaughter of the seventy cannot be justified except upon reasons which point to the annihilation of the race.[25]

John West was one of the most significant newspaper editors in nineteenth-century Australia and perhaps its most talented historian.[26] His assessment of the situation in Queensland is worthy of further consideration. He concluded that the government had embarked on a policy of genocide, one aimed at annihilating the Aboriginal race. This was occurring as a consequence both of the actions of the Native Police and of the government's inaction in the face of widespread settler reprisals. But while this may have been a reasonable response at the time and in the aftermath of the killing of the Wills party at *Cullin-la-ringoe*, West's judgement that the target of the colonists' vengeance was the Aboriginal race itself brings us back to that question of which group we should be considering. There is no doubt that both settlers and government officials were set on annihilating the tribes they thought were implicated in the Wills massacre. But whether their dark ambitions went beyond the particular tribes to the race as a whole is another question altogether. In 1861 over half the Aboriginal population of Queensland was living beyond the reach of the settlers and the Native Police. Some would remain so circumstanced for seventy or eighty years. Meanwhile, back in those districts settled a generation earlier, Aborigines were becoming absorbed into the European economy as pastoral workers, fringe dwellers, prostitutes and most notably as troopers in the Native Police Force. The population continued to decline from disease and deprivation and perhaps at a faster rate than during the period of frontier conflict, without much intervention from the settlers either to hasten or stall the demographic decline.

On the other hand, West clearly appreciated that in November and December 1861 there was a systematic campaign of both settlers and police to kill the Wadja people and probably contiguous tribes as well. This was something more than what Carl Feilberg, editor of the

Cooktown Courier, had called a fitful scheme of 'haphazard little massacres'. During those two months the intention was clearly not just to 'keep the blacks quiet' but to wipe out anyone who might have been even remotely associated with the killing of the Wills party.

The passion for revenge provided the so-called *dolus specialis* that drove the colonists beyond the boundaries of the punitive expedition along the path towards annihilation, if not of the race, then certainly of those groups who inhabited a large area of central Queensland. The governor, Sir G. F. Bowen, recognised the power of the passion for revenge. Writing to his superiors in London he explained that in those days after the Wills massacre 'an uncontrolled desire for revenge took possession of each heart'.[27] A more chilling account of the burgeoning lust for revenge was provided by the prominent English scientist J. B. Jukes, who visited the Queensland coast as part of a surveying and scientific expedition during the 1840s. He was a well-educated, humanitarian man who had

> always joined in reprobating the cause – less injuries sometimes inflicted by civilized, or semi-civilized man, upon the wild tribes of savage life; and many atrocities have doubtless been committed in mere wantonness, and from brutality or indifference. I have always looked, too, with a favourable eye on what are called savages, and held a kind of preconceived sentimental affection for them, that I believe is not uncommon.

However, the experience of seeing one of his shipmates speared wrought a great change in Jukes' feelings. He found himself 'burning with vexation'. A powerful mood 'of mixed rage and grief, and a kind of animal craving for revenge' took possession of his heart. He felt that

> the life of one of my own shipmates, whatever his rank might be, was far dearer to me than that of a wilderness of savages, and that to preserve his life or avenge his death I could willingly shoot a dozen of these black-fellows.[28]

What the events of November and December 1861 in central
Queensland indicate is that the story of frontier conflict was punctuated
with genocidal moments when settlers and police systematically pursued
particular groups of Aborigines with the intention of destroying them.
Such moments occurred in a variety of circumstances: at the end of a
long period of low-scale conflict that the settlers finally decided to bring
to an end 'once and for all', or when the Aborigines killed a larger-than-
usual group of settlers, or when a well-known colonist or women and
children were victims. It was at such moments that the scattered
and sporadic border wars became genocidal. How many genocidal
moments there were must be a matter of speculation. Much detailed
local research still needs to be done.

In her book *Frontier Lands and Pioneer Legends*,[29] Pamela Watson turns her
attention to how the pastoralists gained control of Queensland's Channel
Country and to the consequent fate of the traditional owners – the tribe
or language group known as the Karuwali – and several other peoples,
the Mitaka, the Marrula and the Karanguru, who spoke related languages
and shared ceremonial observances and other cultural traditions. These
groups occupied a large area of about 40 000 square kilometres, covering
the flood plains of the Georgina River or Eyre Creek, the Diamantina
and Farrar's Creek. It is impossible to determine the precontact population, but it may have been between 2000 and 3000.

The pioneer pastoralists arrived in the Channel Country from 1865
onwards and by the late 1870s there were tens of thousands of sheep and
cattle grazing on the unfenced runs. As in other parts of Australia, the
introduced animals had a disastrous impact on the traditional economy,
driving away the native fauna, monopolising and fouling surface water
and eating local shrubs and grasses that were important in the indigenous
diet. Aboriginal resistance to the invasion of white people and their
animals took what was, by the 1880s, the characteristic form of killing,
maiming and running off stock and spearing isolated stockmen. Conflict

which began in the late 1860s persisted for twenty years. Writing of this period, Mary Durack observed that:

> Every traveller brought rumours of increasing trouble and many settlers now openly declared that Western Queensland could only be habitable for whites when the last of the blacks had been killed out – 'by bullet or by bait'.[30]

On the death of the first white man the settlers called in the Native Police, only recently stationed in the tiny frontier outpost of Thargomindah. The mutilated body of the man was found and the local clan dispersed. No questions were asked as to who had committed the crime or why. 'No arrests were made', Durack explained, and the bodies of those shot around a camp at dawn were left to the 'ravages of wild dogs and birds of prey'.[31]

In the early 1970s the distinguished linguist Luise Hercus carried out extensive research in the region and retrieved the old people's stories. She concluded that the turmoil of early white settlement had been an unmitigated tragedy for the clans of the whole Channel Country. There were, she believes, six major massacres, 'mostly well organised, and intended to wipe out whole groups of people'.[32] The Karanguru, whose country was on the lower reaches of what is now called Eyre Creek, were among the main victims of this carnage.

Hercus believes that three of the massacres took place at the time of great ceremonial occasions when large numbers gathered from different tribes at important sites. In 1971 she recorded the reminiscences of old men and women who remembered the stories of the few survivors of what was probably the most devastating attack at Koonchira Waterhole. She explains that as a result of her research, she believes the massacre at Koonchira was organised by police from Andrewilla and took place around 1885, when police were first stationed there. This massacre and the vengeance parties that resulted from the murder of the cook at Kooninghera Waterhole were 'by all accounts well organised':

they appear intended to kill the maximum number of people, men, women and children.[33]

Hercus concludes that by the late 1880s very few Karangura would have been left. The survivors found refuge at the Kilalpannina mission on Cooper Creek. Oral testimony suggests that by the end of the nineteenth century only two old Karungura were at the mission and that they died soon after. Hercus observes that the Karungura ceased to be mentioned in the twentieth-century literature, 'quite simply because they had been wiped out'. Nobody lives now in what was their traditional heartland, along the channels of the Eyre Creek. It is, she writes,

> truly 'dead man's country', but it is also country that once had a rich tradition of mythology, now vanished.[34]

Watson determined that the Karuwali had suffered a similar fate. Writing of a research visit to the Channel Country in 1992, she observes that no descendants were living on their traditional land, although relics of the past persisted across the landscape. A search revealed

> shattered fragments of clay ovens, and the sun glints off shellfish middens; here and there lie discarded quartz tools, and bits of cranium and other human bone can sometimes be found eroding from the sandhills. But the people are absent as far as I could determine.[35]

Watson pursues her theme beyond the events of the killing time and assesses the impact of drastic environmental change following the introduction of sheep and cattle and the devastating consequences of diseases carried into the Channel Country by the squatters and their workers. The almost complete absence of white women in such a remote locality led to the rapid spread of venereal infections, which, unlike other introduced diseases, were normally transmitted consciously and deliberately, impacting both on the victims themselves and on the chance of demographic recovery once the frontier violence had come to an end.

She concludes that the fate of the Karuwali was a consequence of genocidal actions both pursued and permitted by the Queensland government. Her most challenging argument does not relate to the most obvious causes of death but to the fact that by the 1880s the fatal impact of pastoral occupation was manifest to anyone who cared to look, but that nothing was done to ameliorate the consequences of settler occupation of Aboriginal land. Since the south-west was one of the last regions to undergo white settlement in Queensland,

> the opportunity existed there to prevent or minimise the drastic consequences the pastoral industry brought to Aboriginal life on earlier frontiers; to find ways to prevent abduction and assault of black women and children and to attempt to resolve the problem of two competing uses of land. However, no such effort took place, and European appropriation of black land proceeded in the region with the clear knowledge that it would cause devastating and physically destructive changes to the indigenous community.[36]

With this conclusion in mind, Watson believes that the actions, and the inaction, of the Queensland government conformed closely to the principles embodied in article 11/C of the Genocide Convention, which outlaws action 'deliberately inflicting on the group conditions of life calculated to bring about its physical destruction in whole or in part'. In her summary she argues that the results produced by genocide can be identified over much of Queensland, including severe declines in population, the disappearance of some ethnic communities and the reduction of others to a meagre number of scattered survivors. It is valid to conclude, therefore, that

> many small-scale genocides occurred across the country at the time of pastoral settlement. Certainly, the testimony is convincing enough to

suggest that genocide should be suspected of having taken place in situations in which language groups have disappeared, and individuals have lost critical knowledge of their specific ethnic background.[37]

Richard Kimber reaches a similar conclusion about the pertinence of the Genocide Convention as a result of his detailed study of frontier conflict in Central Australia between 1860 and 1895, which is based on years of collecting oral history in both white and black communities, intimate knowledge of the region and more conventional research among the written records.[38] He takes as his region of concern the country lying within a 400-kilometre radius of Alice Springs, which was explored and settled by Europeans between the 1860s and the 1890s – by workers constructing and then running the Overland Telegraph Line, by pastoralists and by prospectors for gold, rubies and mica in the 1880s. The European population, which may have reached 3000 in the period, was made up almost entirely of adult men. Kimber estimates that there were about 4500 Aborigines in the area in the early years of European occupation, made up of the Aranda (Arrernte), Antakininja, Matun, Tara, Anmatjea, Kaititja and Iliaura.

Kimber estimates that introduced diseases – particularly influenza and typhoid – probably killed about 20 per cent of the Aboriginal population, or 900 people, but his conclusions are tentative. He adopts a similar cautious approach when estimating the numbers killed by pastoral workers and the Mounted Police, but concludes that the actual death toll was far higher than official accounts suggest. Somewhere between 650 and 850 people – almost all of them men – were shot by punitive patrols.[39] Kimber believes that the killing, both deliberate and on a large scale, should be considered as genocidal.

There was arguably another genocidal moment in the western Kimberley in 1894 and 1895. It was preceded by increased conflict between squatters and Aborigines, with spearing of sheep and cattle and growing demands from the settlers that the authorities 'do something' to crush the black resistance. In 1893 Francis Connor, the member for East Kimberley in the Western Australian parliament, asserted that the increasing tensions indicated that the central issue at stake was

> simply a question of whether the natives are to have the country or the whites. There is no use putting a tooth in it; that is what it comes down to. It is simply a question of whether we or they are to have this country.[40]

Conflict reached crisis point late in 1894 when the Aboriginal police tracker Jundamarra shot Police Constable William Richardson. Well armed, Jundamarra retreated into the hills and was with a party of Aborigines who shot and killed two stockmen at Windjana Gorge. Settler anxiety intensified. The local police chief, Sub-Inspector Drewry, sought and received permission from the police commissioner in Perth to take whatever steps he thought necessary to deal with the emergency. The result was that between November 1894 and February 1895 three parties of police, Aboriginal trackers and special constables sworn in for the occasion carried out a series of raids on Aboriginal camps throughout the Fitzroy Valley. In his diary the leader of the campaign, Inspector Lawrence, recorded that the three parties shot a total of forty-nine Aborigines. He provided detailed accounts of the dispersals, including the following example:

> On the 6th inst at daylight came on a camp of about thirty natives in bed of margaret river and sent S.P.C. [Special Police Constable] Blythe and five native assistants to disperse them out of the river. Myself and remainder of party took up different positions around camp. The natives seeing the police sprang to their feet, some of them picking up their spears to defend themselves and others started to run in different directions. The police fired on them killing eleven.[41]

Neither in this entry or similar ones did Lawrence indicate that any attempt had been made to make arrests.[42] There was no suggestion that the party in the bed of the Margaret River had been involved in the shooting of the three white men. They were, Lawrence declared, 'a bad hostile lot'.[43]

The police and settler campaign of 1894–95 has been remembered by the local Aborigines, one of whom was recorded in 1979 as saying:

> They were shooting all along this river. We can show you any time, you know. Bones laying just like rubbish. Right along . . . One would go to one side of the river, and another policeman would go to the other side. If the boys jumped over from the other side of the river, they got shot there. Right along, the Fitzroy. If he came alonga big mob of people, he'd just shoot straight in. He shot more people than we got living here.[44]

The settlers in the north-west were delighted by the police action and there was little dissent anywhere in the colony. But Otavious Burt, the permanent head of the Colonial Secretary's department in Perth, who read all the incoming correspondence from the north, commented in private to the premier, Sir John Forrest, in July 1895:

> There can be no doubt from these frequent reports that a war of extermination, in effect, is being waged against these unfortunate blacks in the Kimberley district . . . How often do we read that the Police 'fell in' or 'came up' with a party of natives and then there follows a record of the slain; or the statement that 'they were taught a severe lesson' – and in many cases there is nothing whatever to show that it was the guilty that suffered. Surely this thing is not as it should be.[45]

Neither Forrest, the commissioner of police, nor anyone else for that matter responded to Burt's concerns.

Like John West before him, Burt responded to one of those occasions when parties of police and settlers systematically worked their way through a chosen region for weeks at a time 'dispersing' any Aboriginal camps they came across. Both concluded that this was something more than the usual course of events in the scattered, sporadic and small-scale conflict that accompanied colonial life for the whole nineteenth century. Each man believed that the great loss of life, openly reported but probably exceeded in reality, suggested that at that moment the colonial governments had decided upon a policy of extermination — of what since 1946 we have known as genocide.

NINE

A DYING RACE

ANY DISCUSSION OF GENOCIDE in Australia must take into account the fact that from the 1820s to the 1940s most white people believed the Aborigines were members of a dying race. It is likely that for much of the time this view was held by a substantial − even an overwhelming − majority of the population. The reasons for this belief varied and changed over time, but the central conviction remained the same and was bolstered by the relentless and demonstrable decline of the indigenous population throughout the nineteenth century and into the early twentieth century. Opinion varied as to the extent of human agency in this demographic catastrophe − whether the settlers were, in one way or another, killing the Aborigines or whether they were dying out because of mysterious causes, or at least causes that were beyond human control.

For anyone considering the matter of genocide, several questions need to be considered. Was there an intention to bring about or hasten the Aboriginal demise? Once the deadly prognosis was accepted, was any action taken to try to halt or reverse the process? How did contemporaries respond to the 'passing of the Aborigines'? Did some of them think the colonists were guilty of what today is known as genocide?

The earliest prophecies of doom were abroad in the 1820s. Barron Field, Justice of the New South Wales Supreme Court, published a poem in 1825 on what he believed was the impending 'extermination of the simple race of Australia'.[1] Two years later Anglican archdeacon T. H. Scott wrote a long letter to Governor Darling about the situation of the Aborigines in the colony, casting serious doubt on the value of initiating programs for assistance and amelioration of the tribes within the boundaries of settlement. The low chance of success and likely slow progress, and the rapidity of European expansion, suggested to Scott that the Aborigines would 'be exterminated'.[2] He summarised a report by Richard Sadlier, who had travelled extensively in the recently occupied territory and concluded that the expansion of settlement ensured the Aborigines' 'misery and extinction'. Unless some immediate steps were taken by the colonial government, 'that extinction [would] take place in the course of the next 30 years'.[3]

A similar, but more detailed, assessment of the situation was provided by 'A Gentleman in New South Wales' in a letter to the Methodist Missionary Society in London in October 1826. 'When we look back on the past history of this unhappy race', he lamented, 'we find nothing to afford us consolation'. Looking to the future, there was nothing to relieve 'the fearful foreboding' unless the colony adopted some expedient to 'stay the waste of human life', which for forty years past had been 'diminishing such of the Aborigines as have been within the bounds of our population'. Settlement, the gentleman declared, had been the scourge of the natives, bringing in its train disease, crime, misery and death. 'Wherever we trace the steps of white population', he observed,

we discover the introduction of evil, the diminution of members, the marks of disease, the pressure of want, the physical and moral ruin of this people. If we enquire where are the tribes that once inhabited the places where Sydney, Parramatta, Windsor and other Towns now flourish, What will be the answer? Their existence is but a name. Assemble them and You will find a few miserable creatures, scarcely human in appearance, rise to bear witness that these spots were once peopled by Aborigines'.[4]

If after forty years colonisation had devastated indigenous society, the gentleman continued, there was little indication that things would change in the future, that the same circumstances would not unfold for generations forward as settlement spread slowly over the whole continent. 'If such be the truth', he said,

> the ruin of the Aborigines is inevitable, unless some expedient be devised to stay those evils. Tribe and Tribe must successively endure the same measure of sufferings until the total annihilation of the Natives of New Holland winds up the sad Catastrophe.[5]

Having delivered his chilling prophecy, the gentleman considered what future generations might think of the colonists, who were all fully and inescapably aware of the consequences of their endeavour and yet took no action, adopted no expedient to ameliorate the tragic situation. 'Should such a state of things be realised,' he wrote,

> what will future generations think of our Christianity, of our landed Philanthropy, when our posterity read in the early page of Australian history the misery and ruin which marked our adoption of this land – when they find recorded that our proprietorship to the soil has been purchased at such a Costly Sacrifice of human happiness and life.[6]

Similar grim prognoses became commonplace in the Australian colonies in the 1830s, but not everyone shared the gentleman's moral anguish or sense of urgency about initiating action to circumvent the 'total annihilation of the Natives of New Holland'. Whereas it took forty years in New South Wales before the sentence of death was passed on the Aboriginal tribes, the newer colonies were founded with that expectation in place. Western Australia's first governor, James

Stirling, discussed the matter in a dispatch to the Colonial Office in 1835, declaring that the Aboriginal race must 'gradually disappear as the Country is occupied'. There was little that could be done to stay the process. Neither the 'humane intentions of His Majesty nor the most anxious and judicious Measures of the Local Government' could prevent the ultimate 'Extinction of that Race'.[7] Many colonists dispensed with references to humane intentions and judicious measures, the editor of the *Sydney Herald* declaring in 1838 that any attempt to civilise the Aborigines was futile. They would and 'must become extinct'.[8]

However, like many others in the colonies, the editor saw the process in a global perspective. There was nothing unusual or particularly culpable in the local situation. Indeed, it was 'in the order of nature' that as civilisation advanced, 'savage nations must be exterminated'.[9] The settlers were doing no more than acting out their preordained role in the great global drama of colonisation. The editor of *the Moreton Bay Free Press* observed in January 1852 that the result of all colonisation seemed to show that when a country 'inhabited by savages falls in the progress of civilization to be occupied by a superior race', the fate of its original inhabitants was from that moment sealed.[10]

Similar comments were made again and again in speeches, sermons, letters, books and editorials in all the colonies. 'Your race is doomed', a correspondent to the *Moreton Bay Free Press* declared in 1858 in a rhetorical address to the Aborigines. In fact, he said, the extinction had been sealed since Cook and the history of the world proclaimed it. It was simply the result of 'knowledge over ignorance — light over darkness — civilization over barbarism — the intellectual over the animal'.[11] In a history of Victoria published in the same year, Thomas McCombie observed that when a 'superior race intrudes on savage tribes the latter are slowly exterminated by war, famine and disease'.[12] The Polish expatriate and explorer Paul Strzelecki adopted an equally universal view of the local tragedy, declaring that:

The decrease and final annihilation of the great majority of indigenous races which has followed, and always does follow, the approach of the whites, – is a fact of such historical notoriety, that the melancholy instance of the Australian natives affords but a further corroboration of the fearfully destructive influence which the one race exerts upon the other.[13]

Strzelecki explained that he had inquired into that 'invisible but desolating influence' that operated like a malignant ally of the white man, but the process was in the manner of an inquest of the one race upon the corpse of the other, ending with the verdict of 'Dead by visitation of God'.[14]

Many other commentators saw the hand of God in the process, the Rev. John Dunmore Lang declaring that the passing of the Aborigines was 'a general appointment of Divine Providence'.[15] But even if the Almighty was not implicated, there did appear to be some unknown force at work that was more than the sum of the obvious causes of Aboriginal mortality, such as violence, disease, malnutrition, and so on. The question provoked the curiosity of the young Charles Darwin when he spent time in the colonies in 1837 while voyaging on the *Beagle*. He concluded that there seemed to be 'some mysterious agency at work'.[16] Contemplating the same problem in 1840 from the centre of the empire, the distinguished scholar and Colonial Office official Herman Merivale argued that the Aborigine's decline was not primarily due to the more obvious causes of death, because there were 'deeper and more mysterious causes at work', and indeed that mere contact with Europeans was 'fatal to him in some unknown manner'.[17] Other investigators dealt with the mysterious process by employing a range of metaphors that had the Aborigines 'fading away' or 'fading', 'decaying', 'slipping from life's platform', 'melting like the snow from the summits of the mountains on the appearance of spring',[18] 'sullenly and sadly' retiring to the 'tomb of national and individual existence',[19] or disappearing 'as does the autumnal grass before a bush fire'.[20]

By the middle of the nineteenth century, many colonists had concluded that the Aborigines were dying all over the settled districts and assumed the process would continue. They debated the causes of the demographic disaster and while some deplored what was happening, others thought it a necessary and even desirable development. No-one doubted that colonisation itself was to blame, even if some of the causal links were wrapped in mystery. By seeing the process as part of a universal phenomenon, the settlers were able to avoid moral responsibility for the fate of the Aborigines. This was a colonial characteristic noted by the Royal Navy captain J. L. Stokes, who spent time in Australia in the early 1840s. He found that most people he spoke with were willing to content themselves with the belief that the disappearance of the Aborigines was 'in accordance with some mysterious dispensation of Providence'. Stokes himself was not willing to accept that there was an absence of moral responsibility on the part of the whites. 'I must deny', he declared, 'that it is in obedience to some all-powerful law, the inevitable operation of which exempts us from blame'. The depopulation of countries colonised by the British was, he believed, a 'national crime'.[21]

It is possible to find in each of the colonies people who adopted the same view as Stokes and refused to take comfort from the belief that the Aborigines were being carried off by mysterious forces or in accordance with the will of God. They were almost certainly a minority and their views were not popular. But it is very difficult to find anyone who suggested that colonisation itself should cease, that settlement should be contained in order to save the lives of the tribes who still lived in freedom over half the continent. If, as most colonists agreed, settlement spelt the doom of the Aborigines, it was a price that, almost without exception, they were willing to pay. In fact, the 'disappearance of the black race before the face of the white man' was an inevitable fact to which the settlers 'must of necessity submit as one of the conditions of successful colonization . . .'[22] As the deeply humane John West wrote in his *History of Tasmania* in 1852:

No man can witness the triumph of colonization, when cities rise in the desert, and the wilderness blossoms as the rose, without being gladdened

by the change; but the question which includes the fate of the aborigines – what will become of them? – must check exultation. The black will
invade rights he does not comprehend; seize on stragglers from those flocks,
which have driven off his game; and wound the heel which yet ultimately
treads him to the dust. Such is the process – it is carelessly remarked, that
the native is seen less often . . . At length the secret comes out: the tribe
which welcomed the first settler with shouts and dancing, or at worst
looked on with indifference, has ceased to live.[23]

The rapid population decline, which Darwin had thought in the 1830s
was due to some mysterious agency, was no longer seen in that light in
the second half of the nineteenth century. The change of perception was
largely, if not solely, due to Darwin's own work on evolution and
published in *The Origin of the Species* (1859) and *The Descent of Man* (1871).
A host of followers applied evolutionary theory to society and to the
Aborigines, who were viewed as primitive, stone-age people who were
earlier and less evolved than were Europeans. Their fate was wrought in
the iron laws of evolution; they would inevitably die out, having failed
to survive in the struggle for existence.

The conviction that extinction was inevitable grew even stronger as
the century progressed. Local experience and evolutionary theory
provided mutual confirmation and support. In 1865 the *Brisbane Courier*
noted that in all the colonies the 'almost universal conviction' was that
'no matter what we do, the native race will perish before our
advance . . .'[24] The editor of the *Age* observed in 1881 that it appeared
'to be taken for granted that the Aborigines are doomed'.[25] A correspondent writing to the *Queenslander* in 1880 commented: 'That the race
is doomed is admitted by all who have studied the subject'.[26] In a paper
submitted to an anthropological journal in 1885 on the New South Wales
tribes, A. L. Cameron wrote:

To say that the aboriginal inhabitants of New South Wales, as indeed of the
whole of Australia, are rapidly passing away, is to utter what may be called

a truism. Almost every writer on the subject has borne testimony to their rapid decadence; and even to the uninquiring and little interested, the fact that they are swiftly and surely treading the path to utter annihilation must be evident.[27]

Innumerable other observers added their voices to this dirge of the dying race.

The Australian colonists deeply influenced by social Darwinism had come to accept that, as a consequence of settlement, the indigenous people were dying out and the process would probably continue until it was complete. Some regret was expressed, but in general the impending disappearance was met with equanimity and little sense of moral responsibility. 'All effort to preserve them', wrote the Aboriginal 'expert' Archibald Meston in 1889, 'though creditable to our humanity, is a poor compliment to our knowledge of those inexorable laws whose operations are as apparent as our own existence'.[28] In his letter to the press, A.C.G. adopted a similar view of the matter, remarking that

> those who know the nigger best feel most the impossibility of doing much to ameliorate his condition or protract the existence of his race. This callousness as a rule arises from no lack of sympathy with the blacks, but from a firm conviction that their stage of civilization is too many hundred or perhaps thousand years behind our own to allow their race to thrive side by side with ours.[29]

The Victorian historian A. G. Sutherland observed in 1888 that the colonisation of Australia was a distinct step in human progress 'involving the sacrifice of a few thousand of an inferior race'. It was all beyond individual volition: human beings were 'governed by animal laws which urge them blindly forward upon tracks they scarce can choose for themselves'; they acted under the sway of 'natural laws over which they had no control'.[30] The historian of the pastoral industry, James Collier, argued that there was no question of right or wrong involved in the destruction of Aboriginal society; it was 'simply a question of superiority of race and the greater inherent capability on the part of the whites'.[31]

Popular discourse about struggle and survival of the fittest made it much easier to tolerate the brutal conflict that continued on the remote frontiers of white settlement. Nature itself was 'absolutely and wisely pitiless', the *Age* declared in 1881.[32] Personal violence could be construed as action taken in harmony with the laws of nature, each man's cause that of the white race. Frontiersmen came to consider that it was a duty they owed to themselves and their colour 'to shoot down every black fellow' that came within range of their rifle.[33] Others felt that the violence was unacceptable because it was unnecessary: the fate of the Aborigines was sealed anyway. In 1867 the editor of the *Rockhampton Bulletin* wrote powerfully against 'a ruthless and indiscriminate extermination of the doomed race':

> Their extinction is only a question of time, and no unnecessary cruelty should be used to effect a result which the operation of natural causes will certainly accomplish.[34]

Such tough-minded talk about struggle and racial triumph muted as the twentieth century progressed, but the conviction that the Aborigines were doomed to extinction remained a central feature of Australian life, supported by leading scientists, ethnographers and assorted experts who claimed to understand the Aboriginal situation. No-one was more consistent and emphatic on the question of extinction than Daisy Bates. In a lecture given before Governor-General and Lady Northcote in 1907, she insisted that it should never be forgotten that white Australia was 'dealing with a dying race'. All that could be done was 'to render their passing easier'.[35] In an article in the *Sydney Morning Herald* in 1921 she repeated her message. 'It cannot be too much stressed', she told readers, 'that the Aborigines are a dying race'. In the meeting of civilisation and primitive man, 'the latter must disappear'.[36]

Much the same position was adopted by the celebrated scientist

Baldwin Spencer, who observed in 1899 that within a comparatively short time all that could be done was to gather 'the few remnants of the tribe into some mission station where the path to final extinction may be made as pleasant as possible.'[37] He, too, repeated his prognosis in 1921 when addressing a meeting of the Australian Association for the Advancement of Science. It could, he announced, only be a matter of 'a few years before they are extinct'.[38] W. L. Cleland, the president of the Royal Society of South Australia, addressed his colleagues in 1899, declaring that the Aborigine 'must shortly entirely disappear from the face of the earth, for he is an anachronism and archaic'.[39] In Queensland, Dr Ronald Hamlyn-Harris, the president of the local Royal Society, declared that the native was 'passing at an appalling rate'.[40] In 1928 the professor of pathology at Adelaide University, J. B. Cleland, argued that

> the pure-blooded Australian aborigine is fast dying out. Already over very large areas in the settled parts he has entirely disappeared. With the march of civilization only a few years will see, in all probability, the complete disappearance of pure-blooded natives.[41]

In 1930 Queensland's Chief Protector of Aborigines, J. W. Bleakley, wrote an article entitled 'Can our Aborigines be preserved?', wryly observing that the matter was not a hotly debated question for it seemed 'to be the generally accepted view that the extinction of the Australian Aborigines is inevitable'.[42]

During the nineteenth century, theory and local experience were mutually reinforcing. The Aboriginal population was declining on cue, as the theorists predicted. In district after district, communities noted the passing of the last remaining 'full-blood' of the local tribe. However, in the 1920s and 1930s the situation changed. Quite suddenly, Australian society was faced with the reality of a rapidly growing 'half-caste' population, particularly in Queensland, the Northern Territory and Western Australia. It coincided with a time of anguish about the 'menace of colour' and deep concern about the perpetually blighted prospects for developing the north.

In the forefront of the debate about the 'half-caste problem' were three government officials: Bleakley in Queensland, Dr Cecil Cook in the Northern Territory and A. O. Neville in Western Australia. In his annual report to parliament in 1933, Bleakley expressed his deep worry about the increase of the 'half-caste' population, which in all States had caused 'grave concern'. However, it was, he observed,

> difficult to see how this social blot can be erased as long as the white and black races are allowed in contact, no matter how stringent the laws may be made. Only complete segregation of the black race, which is financially impractical at present, or, as even suggested by some, sterilization of the females, an absolutely unacceptable solution, will prevent the results of intercourse.
>
> The efforts of the Department have in the past been directed to the checking of this evil, by sternly preventing miscegenation, as far as the limited machinery made possible. The marriage of whites and aborigines, unfortunately not discouraged in early years, has been absolutely prohibited, and every encouragement given to these women to marry amongst their own race.[43]

The problem appeared to be most acute in the Northern Territory, where the half-caste population was increasing much more rapidly than the white one. Many half-castes were of mixed Aboriginal and Asian parentage – their very existence a threat to the White Australia Policy. In the opinion of white Territorians, half-castes were, by definition, undesirable members of the community. The administrator of the Northern Territory observed in 1914 that it was freely stated that all half-castes were morally worthless – 'that the taint is in them, and that it must inevitably manifest itself'.[44] But the real danger was much larger than the perceived failings of individuals. Dr Cook spelt it out in a report to the federal government in 1933:

With the rising to maturity of the existing half-caste population and its continued increase at the present rate, it would appear to be a matter of only a few decades before the half-castes equal or exceed in number the white population . . .

If the national ideal of a White Australia is not to be superseded by a modification permitting a coloured north, steps must be taken to limit the multiplication of the hybrid coloured population.

Cook traced out three possible scenarios, each of which appeared undesirable:

(a) The establishment of a predominant and virile coloured population living at white standards, competing on equal terms with the white man in the country and gradually eliminating his competition;

(b) A predominantly coloured population regarded as an inferior section of the community competing with the white on the basis of low wages and . . . rapidly eliminating white labour;

(c) An ever-increasing coloured population of revolutionary frame of mind excluded by statute from industry and maintained on government relief.[45]

In a letter written in 1931 Cook spelt out his fears even more clearly. In the Territory, he explained,

the preponderance of coloured races, the prominence of coloured alien blood and the scarcity of white females to mate with the white male population creates a position of incalculable future menace to purity of race in tropical Australia, and the Federal Government must so regulate its Territories that the multiplication of multi-colour humanity by the mating of Half-caste with alien coloured blood shall be reduced to a minimum. Half-caste females in centres of population where alien races are prominent unfortunately exceed males in number. If this excess is permitted to mate with alien blood, the future of this country may very well be doomed to disaster.[46]

Central, then, to Cook's fears was the large number of single adult males of non-European origin and the considerable population of young part-Aboriginal women who had been brought into the towns as children. It was critical that the lives of these women be controlled. Cook couldn't have been clearer in his objective, explaining that if the 'propagation of the hybrid is to be controlled, either the excess females must be detained for the rest of their lives by the Administration or they must be married to men substantially of European origin'.[47] The government, he insisted, must use every endeavour 'to breed out the colour by elevating female half-castes to white standard with a view to their absorption by mating into the white population'.[48] This experiment in planned breeding was the only method by which the future of the country could be safeguarded 'in the absence of such radical methods as sterilization of the unfit and legalized abortion'.[49]

Cook believed that his policy of breeding out the colour was modern, humane and advanced, and in the circumstances of the time there was an element of truth in this claim. He had quickly taken on board the latest scientific work about racial origins, which postulated that the Aborigines were not a unique and primitive race but were Caucasian in origin, thereby permitting easy intermarriage. It was an idea which directly challenged conventional thinking about the perils of miscegenation and the profound social stigma associated with the establishment of permanent relationships across the caste barrier. The policy was also premised on the improvement of Aboriginal health, education and housing, especially where young half-caste women were concerned, for they had to be prepared for marriage to white men. And in the long run the policy looked forward to the granting of full citizenship to the uplifted half-caste. For all that, the objective of the policy was the biological absorption of the Aboriginal and part-Aboriginal population of north Australia at a time when their numbers were small enough to make the exercise possible.

Cook's activities met with criticism from all sides and never became official federal government policy. In his study of Northern

Territory Aboriginal policy between 1911 and 1938, Tony Austin concluded that Cook's scheme of biological engineering was so extreme that it never received formal endorsement by government. However, 'tacit approval' remained and Cook was given 'no official encouragement to abandon his intention to breed out the colour or "pug-im up white" as the policy was more popularly known by its victims in the North'.[50] A similar assessment was made by Russell McGregor in his book *Imagined Destinies*. While bureaucrats in Canberra were unenthusiastic about schemes for breeding out the colour, 'they were not antagonistic; and Cook was able to develop his policy from Darwin without official hindrance'.[51]

While Cook was seeking to breed out the colour in the Territory, his colleague A. O. Neville was pursuing similar objectives in Western Australia in response to the rapid increase in the half-caste population in the south-west of the State. The Rev. Mr Boxall, spokesman for the Australian Aborigines Amelioration Association, informed the Minister for Aboriginal Affairs in 1933 that while 'the full bloods were dying out', 'the half-castes were breeding like rabbits'.[52] Neville regarded the people of the south-west as 'human flotsam borne upon the waters of ignorance, superstition and indifference'.[53] It was necessary to decide whether they were to be encouraged to intermarry with the white population or remain 'an outcast race which will rapidly become an increasing incubus of the community generally'.[54]

Like Cook, Neville was confident that it would be possible to breed out the colour. 'Eliminate the full blood', he wrote, and permit the white admixture, 'and eventually the race will become white'. In fact, the Aborigines were destined to become absorbed 'in the whites and to emerge as part of the white race'.[55]

Neville was able to gain almost complete control over the part-Aboriginal population as a result of new State legislation in 1936. But he achieved little before his retirement in 1940 due to opposition from a number of quarters and continuing chronic underfunding of the department. Perhaps his most significant achievement was in helping to determine the outcome of the 1937 conference of Commonwealth and State Aboriginal authorities. In a speech to his colleagues, he outlined the thrust of his policy:

> If the coloured people of this country are to be absorbed into the general community, they must be thoroughly fit and educated at least to the extent of the three R's . . . Once that is accomplished there is no reason in the world why these coloured people should not be absorbed into the community. To achieve this end, however, we must have charge of the children at the age of six years; it is useless to wait until they are twelve or thirteen years of age. In Western Australia we have power under the Act to take away any child from its mother at any stage of its life, no matter whether the mother be legally married or not.[56]

During his speech Neville shifted his attention from his own policies to the future of the nation and the Aboriginal place within it. He observed that as a result of improved welfare the indigenous population was increasing. 'What is to be the limit?' he asked rhetorically.

> Are we going to have a population of 1,000,000 blacks in the Commonwealth, or are we going to merge them into our white community and eventually forget that there ever were any Aborigines in Australia?[57]

Neville moved the resolutions that were adopted as policy by all governments represented at the conference:

> That this conference believes that the destiny of the natives of Aboriginal origin, but not of full-blood, lies in their ultimate absorption by the people of the Commonwealth and it therefore recommends that all efforts be directed to that end.
>
> That . . . efforts of all State authorities should be directed towards the education of children of mixed Aboriginal blood at white standards, and their subsequent employment under the same conditions as whites with

a view to their taking their place in the white community on an equal footing with the whites.[58]

The gentleman's letter of 1826 was prophetic. Settlement was the scourge of the natives. The population declined relentlessly for a further 100 years although few colonists shared his anguish and sense of moral responsibility. But the belief that the Aborigines were dying out – a fate ordained by God or nature – had a profound influence on white attitudes. The settlers and their descendants became accustomed to and easy with the idea. When for the first time in the 1920s and 1930s White Australia faced the prospect of Aboriginal survival and demographic recovery, powerful administrators adopted a policy of breeding out the colour – combining progressive welfare measures with controls designed to effect the eventual disappearance of the Aborigines as a people, until Australia would forget they ever existed. The aim was, by definition, genocidal, even if the practice fell far short of the awesome objective.

TEN

'THE SAME MANNER OF LIVING':
ASSIMILATING THE ABORIGINES

FOR 150 YEARS white Australians openly discussed the impending, and, many thought, the inevitable, extinction of the Aborigines. Running parallel with this discourse was the desire and the hope that the Aborigines would adopt both Christianity and European culture, eschewing their own traditions and way of life. There was a common belief that assimilation would be the means of survival, that cultural absorption would ensure physical continuity.

Underpinning all discussion of the matter was the practically universal belief that indigenous culture was inferior, primitive and of little value. Few people thought its disappearance would represent a loss to the world. Many of those who were most concerned about the fate of the Aborigines, who were compassionate and distressed about the immorality of the colonial venture, were deeply committed to the idea of converting the victims both to Christianity and to all those charac-teristics thought essential to civilisation. Such a conversion would be the ultimate justification for colonisation, and compensation for all its attendant hardship and injustice. The Rev. W. Horton wrote to a London-based mission society from Hobart in 1823 declaring:

Yea, justice itself demands that we, who have taken possession of their native soil, and driven them from its most fertile districts, should now extend to them our fostering care to preserve them from extinction, and to impart to them the blessings of civilisation and religion.[1]

The 'Gentleman from New South Wales' expressed his deep concern about the fate of the Aborigines in his letter to the Methodist Missionary Society and then went on to outline his prescription for a more auspicious future. Missionary exertion, he declared, must be employed, because Christianity alone could effect 'a radical, permanent and happy change in this people'. It was the great power which could bring about 'a total change of character, subdue their wildness, overcome their indolence and fix their residence'.[2] Similar ideas were expressed by other advocates of the Aboriginal cause. Among the most eloquent critics of colonial society was the Baptist minister Rev. John Saunders, who delivered a memorable and widely publicised sermon entitled 'The claims of the Aborigines' or 'The duty of the colonists towards the Aboriginal natives of this territory', which duty was to give 'the doctrine of the cross to this most hopeless variety of the human kind'.[3] He called for both repentance and restitution. It is our duty, he told his Sydney congregation,

> to recompense the Aborigines to the extent we have injured them. It is true we cannot make an atonement for the lives which have been taken, neither can we make reparation for the multitudes which have been hastened to the tomb by the profligacy we have taught them, but we can at least bestow upon the survivors the blessings we enjoy. We have a boon in our hands above all price, Christianity, and the numerous comforts which flow from it, and which are comprehended in the expressive word civilization.[4]

Missionaries were quite open about their objective of converting the Aborigines and breaking the bonds that secured them to their own culture and traditions. Members of the New South Wales Society for

Promoting Christian Knowledge Among the Aborigines, founded in 1819, expressed their deep concern about the 'low and wretched condition of our heathen Brethren in these parts of the world'. But considering and 'highly appreciating the Great Advantages and the Very exalted Privileges and inestimable Benefits of Christianity', they felt that as an important and indispensable duty it was incumbent on them 'by every pious and conciliatory means' to recommend to the Aborigines of New South Wales 'the Habits of useful industry and Civilization', and more especially to lead them to an acquaintance with the first principles of Christianity.[5] The committee of the Church Missionary Society instructed their missionary, the Rev. W. Porter, in February 1838 that he should not be

> discouraged at repeated failures and disappointments. These must be expected, and that for a long period, in dealing with a people in such a deplorable state of barbarism, superstition, and ignorance as those with whom you have to do. The habituating them, however, to habits of industry, order and subordination, though by slow and scarcely perceptible degrees, will tend, in combination with the temporal advantages which they will acquire by their intercourse with you, and above all through the grace of the Gospel, to raise them from their present wretched condition, and to form them eventually into well ordered Christian Communities.[6]

Mission objectives remained remarkably constant until well into the twentieth century. In 1908 the Rev. E. Brown of the Weipa mission on Cape York explained that in dealing with the Aborigines the missionaries were always aware of their great duty, which was 'the lifting up of the black race to a higher standard of life, from the animal to the human life'.[7]

The desire to destroy the 'national pattern' of the Aborigines was not confined to missionaries and other religious figures. Governments were involved in the process as well. In instructions given to Governor Darling in 1825, the Colonial Office urged him to take such measures as appeared to be necessary for the indigenous people's 'conversion to the Christian faith and for their advancement in Civilization'.[8] In July 1834 the House of Commons unanimously passed an address to the king praying that he would direct his colonial governors to take action to secure to the native 'due observance of justice' and 'to promote civilization among them, and lead them to the peaceful and voluntary reception of the Christian religion'.[9]

Australian governors had taken up the same project from the early years of settlement. Governor Macquarie believed that it would only require the 'fostering Hand of Time, gentle Means and Conciliatory manners' to bring the poor 'Unenlightened People into an important Degree of Civilization'.[10] The first governor of South Australia, Sir John Hindmarsh, was much more direct when he addressed the resident Aborigines soon after the setters arrived in Adelaide. 'Black Men,' he declared,

> We wish to make you happy. But you cannot be happy unless you imitate white men. Build huts, wear clothes, work and be useful.
>
> Above all things you cannot be happy unless you love God who made heaven and earth and men and all things.
>
> Love white men, Love other tribes of black men. Learn to speak English.[11]

Archdeacon Scott outlined the objectives of the New South Wales government in a letter written in July 1826, explaining that the intention was to civilise and convert to Christianity 'these unhappy beings' and to bring them and their children up 'to the views we entertain of Religion and all its consequences and happy results'.[12]

Central to the task of converting and civilising the Aborigines was the endeavour to control their children and break the ties that bound them to both kin and culture. The project was initiated in the early years of colonisation and continued in one form or another until the middle years of the twentieth century. It involved governments, missionary organisations and individuals acting with varying degrees of magnanimity.

As early as 1810 the policy of appropriating Aboriginal children was being openly advocated in the *Sydney Gazette* by a correspondent calling himself 'A Friend to Civilization'. He urged the necessity of 'adopting as many of the native children as we can procure' in order to facilitate the process of amalgamation.[13] In 1846 a New South Wales clergyman submitted a letter to a Legislative Council select committee on the future of the Aborigines, advocating the removal of children from their parents, an action that would be calculated to 'entirely remodel the character of the rising generation'.[14] Three years later, another prominent settler advocated the establishment of central schools for indigenous children, the purpose of which would be 'to alter in many instances the original bent of the mind' and to supplant their dark superstitions by the 'bright truths of the Gospel'.[15]

Charles Sturt, the noted explorer and colonial official, gave long consideration to the problem of educating indigenous children and their almost universal return to their own people. He appreciated the strong attraction of tribal life and how the boys longed for the moment when they would be free to go where they pleased and 'join in the hunt or the fray', while the girls were already betrothed and compelled to return to husbands in the bush. 'Why therefore should we be surprised', he asked his readers, 'at the desertion of the children from the native schools?'[16]

Despite his sympathetic understanding of traditional society, Sturt was convinced of the need to remove the children from their families and clans. He realised the question was

involved in difficulty, because in my humble opinion, the only remedy involves a violation, for a time at all events, of the natural affections, by obliging a complete separation of the child from its parents; but, I must confess I do not think that any good will result from the utmost perseverance of philanthropy, until such is the case, that is, until the children are kept in such total ignorance of their forefathers, as to look upon them as Europeans do . . .

Eyre was aware that his proposal was a radical one and that it could be thought that it would require too great a sacrifice of feeling, but he argued that it was the duty of the settlers to do that which would 'conduce most of the benefit of posterity'. The injury would only be inflicted on the present generation, 'the benefit would be felt to all futurity'.[17]

By one means or another Aboriginal children were removed from their own people and raised in dormitories on missions, in boarding schools and other institutions. This was true of all the colonies throughout the nineteenth century and well into the twentieth century. They were commonly subjected to strict and regimented regimes, were unable to have contact with their families and were prevented from speaking their languages, often on pain of severe punishment. A missionary in New South Wales in 1827 explained his plans for Aboriginal children in a letter to a colleague. They must be taught the art of cultivation, he explained, because it was only by being constantly employed that their minds would be made 'susceptible of Religious impressions', and by being tied to a particular locality they would 'always be under the inspection of their teachers'.[18]

Poonindie, near Port Lincoln in South Australia, was one of the best-known missions of nineteenth-century Australia, often held up as an example of what could be achieved by Christian instruction. Matthew Hale, the founder of the mission and subsequently Anglican bishop of both Perth and Brisbane, explained that the inmates had to conform strictly to the habits of civilised life. They had 'to be in their own proper sleeping places at night; they had to attend prayers in the house, take their breakfast, dinner, etc. at the proper time, and attend prayers at night'.[19] A contemporary observer wrote approvingly of Hale's simple, kind, firm Christian earnestness: 'teaching, controlling, reproving, governing . . . these children of the bush'.[20]

Given the widespread conviction that Aboriginal children would automatically benefit from living with Europeans in almost any circumstances and be 'uplifted' in the process, it is not surprising that individual colonists and their families 'adopted' Aboriginal children, acquired in a variety of ways but all illustrating the increasing powerlessness of indigenous communities. The greater the disruption the easier it became to detach children from their kin and culture. The practice of taking Aboriginal children began in the earliest years of settlement and was engaged in by members of the colonial elite — governors and clerics and magistrates — and by poorer settlers as well, who could use black children as personal servants, an experience never before available to them.

Aborigines were particularly useful in the bush — even children who had grown up in traditional society could track stray animals, find food and water and navigate across country. They were valuable enough to buy and sell. A north Queensland squatter wrote with concern to the attorney-general in 1869 about the frequent stealing of children. He instanced the case of two men who had stolen several children and taken them to the goldfields to sell. He feared the practice would continue because it paid so well.[21] Five years later the police magistrate at Normanton informed the government that the stealing of 'gins and children from the blacks' was a matter 'of frequent occurrence here'.[22]

Frontier settlers were quite open about their kidnapping activities. For example, the Queensland squatter Wade-Broun explained in his memoirs that early in his career he had been 'anxious to get a young boy' and that the opportunity had presented itself when he 'came upon the rear of a tribe of blacks'. Wade-Broun rode after a boy of about fourteen, pulled him up onto his horse and galloped away. Called 'Captain', the boy remained with his kidnapper for many years and may never have found his way back to his tribe.[23]

Pressing young indigenous children into the workforce was justified by officials and parliamentarians as well as by frontier squatters. In 1886 a select committee of the Western Australian Legislative Council advocated the reduction of the age at which children could be contracted for work from sixteen to ten. Members considered that:

ten years is not too young, as Aboriginal children mature so much more quickly than civilized ones, and it is at that age that habits of thrift and honesty are most easily inculcated. Should they be at liberty to roam about without employment until sixteen they would be useless afterwards.[24]

So much can be drawn from this nineteenth-century material. Clearly it was considered acceptable, and indeed quite normal, to remove Aboriginal children from their extended families. While those who received the children might gain from the transaction in a number of ways, it was always possible to present it as an act of benevolence that would benefit the child, who was being raised up to a higher level of civilisation. The protector of Aborigines at Normanton observed in 1902 that 'most people will tell you that the child is better off with Europeans', although he himself strongly disagreed.[25] Strict discipline and hard work without pay were clearly seen by many people who 'owned' Aboriginal children as part of their tutelage in civilisation. Removal from indigenous society was regarded as being intrinsically and unquestionably a good thing, and absorption into the world of the settlers a benefit bestowed. So it could all be done with the very best of intentions and the younger the child the more likely a good result, an objective greatly enhanced by cutting off all ties between the child and his and her natural parents, relatives, language and culture. The children should be kept, as Eyre advocated, in total ignorance of their forebears.

The relevance of the colonial experience to the current debate about the stolen generations will be obvious. There was clear continuity from colonial practice to twentieth-century practice. Aboriginal vulnerability persisted, preventing communities from resisting demands to surrender their children. What had been ad hoc and individual became bureaucratised and dominated by government departments. The threat from predatory individuals diminished – if not entirely disappearing – while that from police officers and officials increased. Most States passed legislation in the twentieth century that removed Aboriginal parents' common-law rights over their children and transferred them to Protectors, Board or police officers, and this remained the situation in Queensland from 1897 to 1965, Western Australia from 1905 to 1954, South Australia from 1911 to 1923, the Northern Territory from 1911 to 1964 and New South Wales from 1915 to 1940.

It seems likely that more children proportionately were taken from their families in the first half of the twentieth century than had been the case in the nineteenth century, but the lack of relevant colonial statistics makes close comparison difficult. There was the same conviction among white Australians that children would benefit as a consequence of removal, that it was better done at an early age and better still if all contact with kin and culture was permanently severed. So powerful was this conviction and so deeply entrenched in European thinking that many of those involved in removing children were genuinely convinced that the project was a humane one enlivened by good intentions, regardless of how distressing the execution might be. It enabled the whole program of the Protector of Aborigines, Dr Cecil Cook, to breed out the colour in the Northern Territory to be pursued using powers conferred by an ordinance that allowed the Chief Protector of Aborigines to 'undertake the care, custody, or control of any aboriginal or half-caste' if in his opinion it was 'necessary or desirable in the interests of the aboriginal or half-caste to do so'.[26] Twentieth-century administrators often adopted the same position as that of Charles Sturt, who, as we have seen, believed it was justifiable to violate the 'natural affection' of children and parents because it would be to the benefit of posterity. On his retirement in 1944, A. O. Neville, Chief Protector of Aborigines in Western Australia, defended his policy of biological absorption, explaining:

> The native must be helped in spite of himself! Even if a measure of discipline is necessary it must be applied, but it can be applied in such a way as

to appear to be gentle persuasion . . . the end in view will justify the means employed.[27]

As stated earlier, the 1997 report of the Human Rights Commission into the separation of Aboriginal and Torres Strait Islander children from their families, *Bringing Them Home*, concluded, controversially, that the policies pursued by Australian governments from the early twentieth century to the 1960s constituted crimes against humanity. Even more to the point was their discussion about genocide, which concluded that:

> The policy of forcible removal of children from indigenous Australians to other groups for the purpose of raising them separately from and ignorant of their culture and people could properly be labeled 'genocidal' in breach of binding international law from at least 11 December 1946 . . . The practice continued for almost another quarter of a century.[28]

The report advanced three main arguments in support of its case. The children were removed because they were seen as being members of a distinct group who, if they remained with their own people, would acquire their culture and traditions. Among policy-makers and administrators there was an intention to destroy the group 'in whole or in part'. Indeed, the inquiry's research revealed that the predominant aim of child removals was the absorption or assimilation of the infants into the wider, non-indigenous community so that 'their unique cultural values and ethnic identities would disappear, giving way to models of Western culture'.[29] The third avenue of argument led to a consideration of mixed motives and good intentions and whether the Convention applied in cases where the destruction of a particular group and its family institutions was believed to be 'in the best interests of the children or where the child removal policies were intended to serve multiple aims'.[30] The authors of the report observed that:

Through much of the period beginning around the middle of the nineteenth century and persisting until the repeal of overtly discriminatory legislation in the 1960s, a key objective of the forcible removal of Indigenous children was to remove them from the influence of their parents and communities, to acculturate them and to socialise them into Anglo-Australian values and aspirations. Other objectives included education of the children to make them 'useful' and 'worthy' citizens, their training for labour and domestic service, their protection from malnutrition, neglect or abuse, the reduction of government support for idle dependants and the protection of the community from 'dangerous elements'.[31]

Having outlined all the differing objectives that informed the removal policies over the years, the commissioners concluded that diversity of aim did not necessarily undermine the charge of genocide.[32]

I argued in Chapter Nine that the policies of Cook and Neville in the 1930s had genocidal objectives and that both men were quite open about their desire to 'breed out the colour'. Policies pursued by subsequent ministers and officials in the 1950s need to be dealt with separately. The attempt to coordinate policies across the federation, initiated at the 1937 conference of Aboriginal Affairs ministers, was frustrated by the outbreak of the Second World War. A second conference planned for 1939 was never held, so new policy prescriptions were delayed until a meeting of State and federal ministers in 1951.

Although only fourteen years separated one meeting from the other, the ambient intellectual climate had undergone dramatic changes. Knowledge of the Holocaust and of German policies in the occupied territories had totally undermined the validity of the whole prewar structure of racial science and sociology. Eugenics had been condemned by association. The new United Nations coordinated campaigns to complete the destruction of the intellectual credibility of the concept of race. The European empires were falling to pieces and new nations emerged in Asia and Africa. The Universal Declaration of Human Rights upheld the cause of human equality regardless of racial or ethnic origin. For many people in the postwar world, the rhetoric of people like Neville and Cook was not just mistaken and outmoded but also embarrassing. The new policy objective was assimilation, which was strongly promoted by Paul Hasluck, who became Minister of Territories in 1951 and was therefore responsible for Aborigines in the Northern Territory. In reporting to parliament on the 1951 meeting of ministers, Hasluck remarked that assimilation meant

> in practical terms, that, in the course of time, it is expected that all persons of aboriginal blood or mixed blood in Australia will live like white Australians do.[33]

The conference itself was more specific, asserting that assimilation meant that all Aborigines would

> attain the same manner of living as other Australians, and . . . live as members of a single Australian community enjoying the same rights and privileges, accepting the same customs and influenced by the same beliefs, as other Australians.[34]

Any assessment of Aboriginal policy in the 1950s must, then, address the question of assimilation as well as the ideas and objectives of its major architect, Paul Hasluck.

Hasluck had been involved in Aboriginal affairs in Western Australia before the Second World War. In the 1930s he had written a powerful series of articles about the mixed-blood Aboriginal community in the south-west of the State, published in the *West Australian* in July 1936. The headlines used to introduce the articles were symptomatic of what was to follow:

HALF-CASTE PROBLEM
BIG RISE IN NUMBERS
CAMPS SWARMING WITH CHILDREN[35]

Hasluck was clearly impressed by the rapid increase in the community and the large size of the families. 'Children swarmed in the huts and around the camping grounds', he observed:

> unwashed children badly in need of handkerchiefs. Women could be seen nursing one infant and well advanced towards another. Those were typical sights.[36]

There was no doubt about his concern and compassion for the poverty-stricken conditions of the Aboriginal camp dwellers and the discrimination they experienced in the small rural towns, which made it impossible for them to be 'anything but pariahs, dwellers in huts, breeders of a separate caste.'[37] He was particularly interested in the children, who, he said, had no chance to grow up as anything but 'gypsy-like outcasts'.[38] They were the section of the community that, for Hasluck,

> caused most alarm and gives ground for strongest hope. They might be able to profit from a chance to do better for themselves, but no chance is given. Today they are swarming about the native camps without proper care. Many of them – laughing, ragged urchins, keen in intelligence – are almost white and some of them are so fair that, after a good wash, they would probably pass unnoticed in any band of whites.[39]

Hasluck was strongly in favour of assimilation – and just as strongly opposed to the establishment of segregated settlements, which held out the prospect of a

> strictly isolated group of 'foreign' people, multiplying themselves on biologically unsound lines, going on and on without getting anywhere.[40]

He favoured immediate help to families, the establishment of schools where the children could be prepared to enter the community, and assistance to help some of the 'better families to leave their aboriginal environment at once'. It would require patience, but it would mean, too,

> the passing into the community of some hundreds of valuable workers and the giving of a chance to a submerged people; in two generations there should be no half-caste problem.[41]

That, then, was the way to deal with the half-caste problem, 'an embarrassing nuisance which grows worse every year'.[42] The half-caste should be given rights and privileges by which he 'might be encouraged to separate himself from aboriginal associations and gradually join the whites'.[43]

Many of the ideas expressed in Hasluck's prewar journalism emerged again when he entered federal politics and assumed responsibility for Aboriginal affairs in the Northern Territory, taking on the task of co-ordinating policy throughout the country. The Aboriginal population, he told his parliamentary colleagues in 1950, was 'a serious but not a frightening problem'. Indigenous people constituted a social group within, but not of, the community. Therefore, he concluded, the group could 'and must be managed'.[44] And that was possible in Australia because the local 'race relations problem' was softened by the 'big disproportion of numbers between the two races'. There was no uncertainty about 'who will swallow whom'.[45]

Hasluck had no doubt about the eventual destination of the indigenous population, which was already in transition from traditional society to citizenship within white Australia. That was what advancement meant. In its transitional stage Aboriginal society had no particular virtue. It was a 'scattered minority' that seemed bound to 'lose gradually year by year any prospect of continuing as a separate and assertive group'.[46] Here and there throughout the continent, he told a national conference in 1959, there are crumbling groups of aboriginal people bound together by ancient tradition and kinship and living under a fading discipline . . . the tattered threads of kinship . . . None of this can be identified as a society in the same way as the rest of Australia can be identified as a society.[47]

But the perceived fragility of Aboriginal society was an advantage. The more it crumbled the easier it would be to mingle its fragments with the rest of Australian society.[48]

The separate social organisation had largely broken down, except for 'a handful of tribes in some remote desert areas'.[49] Native welfare was, therefore, a social problem, not a racial one, which related to the way in which two groups of people of different race could live in the same community while 'maintaining their separateness as a group'. In Australia, Aboriginal disadvantage must be treated as a matter relating to the lives of individuals who had to be given greater assistance, the better to enable them to live the best life of which they were capable in order that they might eventually find 'a fitting place as members of the Australian community'.[50] Consequently, the coloured people who lived in Australia

should not be regarded as a class but as part of the general community whenever and as soon as their advancement in civilisation permits them to take their place on satisfactory terms as members of the community.[51]

Assimilation, then, governed 'all other aspects of native affairs administration'.[52] In the long run it would mean that after many generations the Aboriginal people would 'disappear as a separate racial group'. The force of numbers, Hasluck observed, was against them and the history of other lands had shown that a preponderant population had a 'very great capacity to absorb into itself minority elements', although he hoped that the Aborigines would carry 'a proud memory of their own ancient origin'.[53]

However, Aboriginal historical memories should not obstruct the path to assimilation. Anyone who promoted race consciousness and race separateness was working against its early realisation. And so Hasluck sought to break down 'that form of race consciousness' that tried to insist on racial differences and that, when involving Aborigines, stemmed not from pride in themselves 'but resentment against others'.[54] In a speech to parliament in 1955 he explained that he had

> noticed in the last year or two, the growth of what I consider an undesirable tendency in native welfare matters in Australia, and that is a tendency towards the growth of race consciousness among the Aboriginal people themselves, particularly among those who have advanced a little in the world, who have had a European type of schooling, who have got European occupations, and who are still not accepted. They are drawing into racial groups.[55]

Hasluck feared that development, realising it would mean 'the whole of our policy will have been defeated'.[56] He feared what the outcome would be if assimilation did not succeed. There would be the build-up of

> an ever-increasing body of people who being a separate caste, and who live in Australia but are not members of the Australian community. We shall create a series of minority groups who live in little bits of territory of their own.[57]

Paul Hasluck was probably the most able administrator of Aboriginal Affairs during the first sixty years of the twentieth century. He significantly raised the profile of that part of his portfolio and oversaw a considerable increase in expenditure in the Northern Territory and a corresponding improvement in service delivery. He sought to remove obstacles that prevented the gradual achievement of citizenship by Aborigines, and he was more aware than many of his contemporaries of international disquiet about the status of indigenous people in Australian society.

But his whole emphasis was on encouraging individuals and families to break away from their communities and become separately absorbed in white Australia. Aboriginal advancement would come at the price of identity and solidarity. In the long run he hoped that, with the success of assimilation, Aborigines would achieve equality as individuals but would no longer belong to a caste — to a separate and assertive group. After all, he felt there was no doubt as to who would swallow whom. And he knew this was a desirable, necessary and progressive end. It would conduce most to the benefit of posterity.

So with Hasluck we meet again the paradox that was apparent through a century and a half of colonial and national history: that the individuals who were best informed about, more interested in and most concerned and compassionate about the plight of the Aborigines were the leading advocates of their conversion to Christianity, their adoption of Western ways, their assimilation into settler society, their abandonment of their culture and traditions. That appeared to be what benevolence dictated. They were people who, for what they considered to be the very best reasons, wished, in the words of Raphael Lemkin, to see the disappearance of the national pattern of indigenous Australia and the imposition of the national pattern of the colonists and their descendants. It was all a matter of progress and improvement.

But how do the removal of children and the adoption of assimilationist policies after the Second World War relate to the question of genocide? To answer this question, it is necessary to return to the intense debates of 1947 and 1948 that hammered out the details of the Genocide Convention.

CONCLUSION

THE PRACTICE OF removing children from one group and transferring them to another was taken very seriously during the debates that led up to the Genocide Convention. It was the one aspect of what was originally conceived of as cultural genocide that survived the drafting process.

In his speech urging its adoption, the Greek delegate, Pierre Vallindas, argued that the forced transfer of children could be as effective a means of destroying a human group as the imposition of measures to prevent births or inflict conditions likely to cause death.[1] The influential Venezuelan diplomat, Dr V. M. Perez Perozo, spoke about the acceptance by the Sixth Committee of the significance of the transfer of children. This acceptance, he said, gave implicit recognition to the fact that a group could be destroyed even though individual members of it 'continued to live normally without having suffered physical pain'. The clause, he observed,

> had been adopted because the forced transfer of children to a group where they would be given an education different from that of their own group, and would have new customs, a new religion and probably a new language,

173

was in practice tantamount to the destruction of their group, whose future depended on that generation of children. Such transfer might be made from a group with a low standard of civilization and living in conditions both unhealthy and primitive, to a highly civilized group as members of which the children would suffer no physical harm, and would indeed enjoy an existence which was materially much better; in such a case there would be no question of mass murder, mutilation, torture or malnutrition; yet, if the intent of the transfer were the destruction of the group, a crime of genocide would undoubtedly have been committed.[2]

If we apply Dr Perez Peroso's definition of genocide to Australia, the removal of children by governments, churches and individuals over generations would have to be seriously considered as genocidal in effect, if not necessarily in intention. It allows us to understand the reason for the sharp disagreements apparent when different people seek to understand the same events, why the removal of children can be interpreted on the one hand as a well-meaning endeavour to give indigenous children a better life and greater opportunities, and on the other as part of a genocidal project to undermine Aboriginal society. The argument would benefit from a consideration of the critical matter of intent; we should ask the question: 'What did the participants believe they were doing?' When they were quite consciously trying to breed out the colour in the name of White Australia, the charge of genocide has to be taken very seriously. When the motives were much more mixed and the emphasis was on what was thought – often erroneously – to be in the best interests of the child, we move much further away from genocidal intention.

While members of the UN committees were sensitive to the impact of child removal, so recently perpetrated by the Nazi regime in the occupied territories, they showed far less concern for the consequences of policies of assimilation. That, too, can be understood by considering the ambient intellectual and political environment. The new United Nations showed far less concern about minority rights than its predecessor, the League of Nations, had done. The Minority Treaties of the

1920s and 1930s were widely seen as having failed to achieve any positive results. In the 1940s the emphasis was on the rights of individuals – and the rights of states. Assimilation was frequently equated with modernity. Ethnicity was associated with backward societies, remote regions, outmoded social forms. Assimilationist policies were strongly favoured by the many new and emerging states that sought to play down difference in the name of nation-building. Australia's assimilationist policies were very much a product of their time and it is unlikely that the international jurists, officials and politicians who framed the Genocide Convention would have thought these policies should come under its aegis.

Even Raphael Lemkin, who was so committed to seeing cultural genocide included in the Convention, did not regard assimilation as a major problem. In the discussion of his draft convention he observed that cultural genocide related to drastic methods aimed at the 'rapid and complete disappearance of the cultural, moral and religious life of a group of human beings'. It was, he explained, much more serious than 'a policy of forced assimilation by moderate coercion'.[3]

Many of the speakers who contributed to the debate within the UN made similar remarks. For example, the Polish delegate, P. R. Rudjinski, argued that the purpose of the proposed convention was not to interfere with 'the natural evolution of humanity or the inevitable absorption of certain minority groups into the national whole', but rather to prevent the violence, persecution and excesses that had recently aroused the conscience of humankind.[4] In the Sixth Committee the Brazilian delegate, Gilberto Amado, warned his colleagues that care should be taken 'when dealing with new countries' not to favour minority movements that opposed 'the legitimate efforts made to assimilate the minorities by countries in which they were living'.[5] Quintin Paredes from the Philippines concurred, warning that nations must retain the right to 'integrate the different elements of which they were composed into a homogeneous whole'.[6] Iran's Dr Djalal Abdoh wondered whether all cultures, 'even the most barbarous, deserved protection', doubting that the assimilation 'resulting from civilizing action of a State' constituted genocide.[7] Brazil's

Ramiro Guerreiro warned that in the desire to punish genocide it was important not to give encouragement 'to the formation of minorities in new nations' that had been formed and developed by immigration. Such minorities might make use of the Convention to resist the country's 'legitimate desire that they should assimilate'.[8] For his part, the Egyptian delegate to the Sixth Committee, Dr W. Raafat, did not want to hamper 'a reasonable policy of assimilation which no State aiming at national unity could be expected to renounce'.[9] It is significant that no-one condemned assimilationist policies or argued that they had genocidal implications.

Given the strong support for assimilation in the United Nations in the 1940s, it is most unlikely that any indigenous minority would have been able to find support for the argument that such policies were, by definition, genocidal. We can assume that, had he known of it, Lemkin would have accepted as appropriate Paul Hasluck's drive for assimilation.

Although the clauses concerning cultural genocide were rejected during the drafting process, numerous delegates spoke powerfully about the phenomenon itself. Perez Perozo observed that a group could be deprived of its existence not only as a result of the physical destruction of its members but also through the 'destruction of its specific traits', the loss of which would lead to 'the dissolution of its unity, even though no attempt had been made on the life of its members.[10] The Chinese delegate, Tsien Tan, remarked that although cultural genocide seemed less brutal than physical or biological genocide it might be even more harmful, since it worked 'below the surface and attacked the whole population, attempting to deprive it of its ancient culture and to destroy its very language'.[11]

However, many speakers felt that the protection of language, religion and culture should be dealt with under the more general rubric of human rights rather than the Genocide Convention, and eventually this happened with the ratification of the International Covenant on Civil and Political Rights in 1966. Minority rights were referred to in article 27, which provided that individual members 'shall not be denied the right in community with other members of their group to enjoy their own culture, to profess and practise their own religion or to use their own language'.[12] The article has been widely viewed as supplementing the Genocide Convention. The earlier Convention guaranteed the rights of minorities to continued physical existence; article 27 provided for the survival of minority cultures and the right to an identity.

While article 27 was phrased in a cautious – and negative – manner, it has assumed much greater significance since 1966 and has acquired direct local relevance since Australia ratified the Covenant in 1980. The general view now is that governments are expected to do much more than leave their minorities alone, that active and sustained intervention is required to create the conditions that will allow them to survive. The overseeing authority, the UN Human Rights Committee, issued a statement in 1994 clarifying the scope of article 27, which placed participating govern-ments under an obligation to ensure that the existence and exercise of the right to enjoy one's culture was 'protected against denial or violation, particularly against acts of state, whether through its legislative, judicial or administrative authorities'. The capacity to enjoy that culture, the committee observed, might well depend on a way of life 'closely asso-ciated with territory and the use of its resources', on the availability of those resources or on assistance from the government to facilitate the preservation of traditional languages and traditions.[13]

For most of the time since 1788 white Australians have shown no desire or will to ensure the survival of the Aborigines as a people. They widely assumed that the indigenous population would die out, taking their culture, languages and traditions with them. When the colonists argued about the conflict out on the frontiers of settlement, few lamented the loss of languages or oral traditions even while they condemned the brutality of it all. They often regretted the loss of life, but rarely referred to the irretrievable loss of culture. It was common to welcome 'the passing of the Aborigines' as an indicator of colonial progress, a measure of achievement.

Even the intense ethnographic interest of the late nineteenth and early twentieth centuries was stimulated by the expectation that the tribes were both dying out and losing their culture. Research was conducted with a sense of urgency, with the conviction that the unique Stone Age culture was important to scholars because it was archaic, doomed and far removed from contemporary civilisation. Aborigines who had adapted to the world of the colonists held no interest for the men of science.

The most compassionate of the settlers, those most engaged with indigenous society, were very often the strongest promoters of the duty to Christianise and civilise, to draw the subjects of their interest away as quickly and completely as possible from their own traditions and way of life, to take the children away to facilitate the process – and all with a clear conscience.

When it became apparent in the 1920s and 1930s that the part-Aboriginal population, contrary to expectations, was rapidly increasing, few white Australians applauded the dramatic demographic turnaround. Even a humanitarian like Hasluck saw it not as an achievement but as a problem. Though they differed in their preferred method, both Neville and Hasluck looked forward to the time when there would be no more Aborigines – or at least no recognisable or assertive community – either because they had been bred out of existence or absorbed individually into white society. Hasluck promoted assimilation by referring to two central, widely supported national goals – national unity and social equality – that he believed were incompatible with the continued existence of a self-conscious Aboriginal population secure in its identity.

Assimilation has gone out of fashion – or rather the word is no longer commonly used – but the desire to absorb the indigenous people into the nation is still strong. It was one of the threads that ran through the reconciliation movement, although there were others that were woven in a contrary direction.

If asked whether they favoured the continued survival of Aborigines and Torres Strait Islanders as distinct peoples, most Australians would probably say yes. But it is far from clear whether they would support equally well measures that may be necessary to ensure that this survival occurs — such things as recognition of customary law, self-government, regional agreements, and constitutional definition of indigenous rights.

Without them, the long-heralded, often-anticipated disappearance of the Aborigines may yet come to pass.

NOTES

Abbreviations

ALJR – Australian Law Journal Reports
CO – Colonial Office
CSO – Colonial Secretary's Office
FCA – Federal Court of Australia
HRA – Historical Records of Australia
ML – Mitchell Library
TSA – Tasmanian State Archives
UN – United Nations

Introduction

1   *Sun Herald*, 8 Oct. 2000.
2   'The World Today', ABC Radio, 23 Feb. 2001.
3   A. G. L. Shaw (ed.), *Van Diemen's Land*, THRA, Hobart, 1971, p. 56.

Chapter 1:
Two Canberra cameos

1   UN General Assembly, Third Session, Official Records, 21 Sept.–12 Dec. 1948, p. 822.
2   Australia, House of Representatives 1949, *Debates*, vol. 202, pp. 1864–5.
3   ibid., p. 1874.
4   ibid., p. 1876.
5   Written Submission on the Matter of an Application for a Writ of Mandamus, 7 Aug. 1998, no. SC457 of 1998.
6   See *Nulyarimma v Thompson* (1999) FCA 1192.

7   Affidavit no. 2 of Wadjularbinna Nulyarimma, affirmed 8 July 1998, Supreme Court of the ACT, p. 1.
8   ibid., p. 2.
9   ibid.
10 ibid., p. 5.
11 ibid.

Chapter 2:
The Genocide Convention

1   R. Lemkin, *Axis Rule in Occupied Europe*, Carnegie Endowment for International Peace, Washington, 1944.
2   ibid., p. 79.
3   ibid.
4   E. Osmanczyk (ed.), *Encyclopedia of the United Nations*, 2nd edn, Taylor & Francis, New York, 1990, p. 328.
5   UN, *Study of the Question of the Prevention and Punishment of the Crime*

of Genocide, E/CN.4/Sub.2/416, 1978, p. 8.

6 UN, *Treaty Series*, vol. 78, pp. 280–1.

7 UN, *Draft Convention on the Crime of Genocide*, E/447, p. 16.

8 UN, Ad Hoc Committee on Genocide, 12th meeting, E/AC.25/SR.12.

9 L. J. Le Blanc, 'The intent to destroy groups in the Genocide Convention', *American Journal of International Law*, vol. 78, 1984, pp. 371–2.

10 P. N. Drost, *The Crimes of State*, Sythoff, Leyden, 1959, vol. 1, p. 82.

11 UN, *Draft Convention*, op. cit., p. 23.

12 UN, Ad Hoc Committee on Genocide, E/AC.25/3, p. 6.

13 Quoted by Le Blanc, op. cit., p. 378.

14 ibid., p. 371.

15 Lemkin, op. cit., p. 91.

16 UN, *Draft Convention*, op. cit., p. 27.

17 Quoted by Drost, op. cit., p. 1.

18 UN, *Draft Convention*, op. cit., pp. 6–7.

19 ibid., p. 27.

20 UN, *Study of the Question*, op. cit., p. 23.

21 Drost, op. cit., p. 87.

22 UN, Ad Hoc Committee, 7 April 1948, E/AC.25/12, p. 23.

23 ibid.

24 UN, *Draft Convention*, op. cit., p. 25.

25 ibid.

26 Drost, op. cit., p. 86.

27 Quoted by H. Fein in *Genocide: A Sociological Perspective*, Sage, London, 1990, p. 13.

28 Quoted by Fein, ibid., p. 16.

29 F. Chalk & K. Jonassohn, *The History and Sociology of Genocide*, Yale University Press, New Haven, 1990, p. 23.

30 Fein, op. cit., p. 24.

31 ibid., p. 79.

32 I. Charny, 'Towards a generic definition of genocide', in G. J. Andreopoulos (ed.), *Genocide: Conceptual and Historical Dimensions*, University of Pennsylvania Press, Philadelphia, 1994, p. 80.

33 Chalk & Jonassohn, op. cit., p. 36.

34 A. Palmer, Colonial Genocides: The Aborigines of Queensland (1840–1897) and the Hereros of South West Africa (1884–1906), Ph.D. thesis, University of London, 1993, p. 68.

35 R. W. Smith, 'Human destruction and politics', in M. Dobkowski & I. Wallimann (eds), *Genocide and the Modern Age*, Greenwood, New York, 1987, p. 23.

36 T. Barta, 'After the Holocaust: consciousness of genocide in Australia', *Australian Journal of Politics and History*, vol. 31, no.1, 1984, pp. 154–61.

37 ibid., p. 156.

38 ibid.

39 ibid.

40 T. Barta, 'Relations of genocide: land and lives in the colonization of Australia', in Dobkowski & Wallimann, op. cit., p. 238.

41 ibid., p. 239.

42 *Coe v. Commonwealth of Australia* (1979) 53 ALJR 412.

43 World Council of Churches, *Justice for Aboriginal Australians*, Australian Council of Churches, Sydney, 1981, p. 8.

44   H. Wootten, *Report of the Inquiry into
     the Death of Malcolm Charles Smith*,
     AGPS, Canberra, 1989, pp. 76–7.

45   *Bringing Them Home*, Human Rights
     & Equal Opportunity Commission,
     Sydney, 1997, p. 273.

46   ibid., p. 275.

47   C. Tatz, *Genocide in Australia*,
     Aboriginal Studies Press, Canberra,
     1999, p. 6.

48   In the Matter of an Application for
     a Writ of Mandamus, 18 Dec. 1998,
     ACTSC 136 ACTR9 78.

49   *Nulyarimma v. Thompson*, ibid.,
     pp. 4–5.

50   ibid., p. 6.

Chapter 3:
An extraordinary calamity

1   W. Tench, *Sydney's First Four Years*,
     ed. L. F. Fitzhardinge, Angus &
     Robertson, Sydney, 1961, p. 146.

2   D. Collins, *An Account of the English
     Colony in New South Wales* [1798], ed.
     B. H. Fletcher, A & A Reed, Sydney,
     1975, vol. 1, p. 53.

3   *Historical Records of New South Wales*,
     vol. 1, 1783–92, Govt Printer,
     Sydney, 1892, p. 308.

4   J. Hunter, *An Historical Journal of
     Events at Sydney and at Sea,
     1787–1792* [1793], Angus &
     Robertson, Sydney, 1968, p. 93.

5   Collins, op. cit., vol. 1, p. 496.

6   Tench, loc. cit.

7   J. R. Smith, *The Speckled Monster*,
     Essex Records Office, Chelmsford,
     1987, p. 43. See also D. R. Hopkins,
     Princes and Peasants, University of
     Chicago Press, Chicago, 1983.

8   Smith, op. cit., p. 53.

9   ibid., p. 46.

10   J. H. L. Cumpston, *The History of
     Smallpox in Australia, 1788–1908*,
     Commonwealth Quarantine Service,
     Melbourne, 1914.

11   ibid., p. 2.

12   N. G. Butlin, *Close Encounters of the
     Worst Kind: Modelling Aboriginal
     Depopulation and Resource Competition
     1788–1850*, Working Paper in
     Economic History no. 8, ANU,
     Canberra, 1982.

13   ibid., p. 27.

14   ibid.

15   N. G. Butlin, *Our Original Aggression:
     Aboriginal Populations of Southeastern
     Australia 1788–1850*, Allen &
     Unwin, Sydney, 1983.

16   ibid., p. 21.

17   Tench, op. cit., p. 144.

18   ibid., p. 22.

19   ibid., p. 175.

20   N. G. Butlin, *Macassans and Aboriginal
     Smallpox: The 1789 and 1829
     Epidemics*, Working Paper in
     Economic History no. 22, ANU,
     Canberra, 1984, p. 20.

21   T. Duncan, 'Aboriginal theory lacks
     evidence', *Bulletin*, 5 Feb. 1985.

22   C. Wilson, 'History, hypothesis and
     fiction', *Quadrant*, vol. XXIX, no. 3,
     March 1985, p. 28.

23   J. Campbell & A. Frost, 'Aboriginal
     smallpox: the 1789 and 1829
     epidemics', *Historical Studies*, vol. 21,
     no. 84, April 1985; J. Campbell,
     'Smallpox in Aboriginal Australia: the
     early 1830s', *Historical Studies*, ibid.

24   J. Campbell, 'Whence came the
     pox?', *Age Monthly Review*, vol. 3,
     no. 10, Feb. 1984, p. 20.

25 See for instance Butlin, *Macassans*, op. cit., p. 18.
26 Butlin, *Our Original Aggression*, op. cit., p. 20.
27 A. Frost, *Botany Bay Mirages*, Melbourne University Press, Carlton, 1994.
28 Butlin, *Our Original Aggression*, op. cit., p. 21; Butlin, *Macassans*, op. cit., p. 334.
29 Frost, op. cit., pp. 200–1.
30 *Journal of American History*, vol. 86, March 2000.
31 ibid., pp. 1555–7.
32 ibid., pp. 1556–7.
33 ibid., p. 1580.
34 E. Geissler & J. E. van Courtland Moon (eds), *Biological and Toxin Weapons: Research, Development and Use from the Middle Ages to 1945*, Oxford University Press, Oxford, 1999, p. 26.
35 Fein, op. cit., pp. 1568–72.
36 ibid., p. 1570.
37 ibid., p. 1568.
38 ibid.

Chapter 4:
Tasmania: A clear case of genocide?
1 Tasmania, House of Assembly 1993, *Parliamentary Debates*, no. 11, 15–17 June, p. 3175.
2 18 June 1993.
3 Tasmania, *Parliamentary Debates*, op. cit., pp. 3421–2.
4 L. L. Robson, *A History of Tasmania*, Oxford University Press, Melbourne, 1983, vol. 1, p. vii.
5 N. G. Butlin, *Economics and the Dreamtime*, Cambridge University Press, Melbourne, 1993, p. 134.

6 R. Hughes, *The Fatal Shore*, Pan, London, 1987, p. 120.
7 Fein, op. cit., p. 11.
8 L. Kuper, *Genocide*, Penguin, Harmondsworth, 1981, p. 40.
9 W. Churchill, 'Genocide: towards a functional definition', *Alternatives*, vol. XI, 1986, p. 421.
10 J. Diamond, 'In black and white', *Natural History*, Oct. 1988, p. 257.
11 F. Mazian, *Why Genocide?*, Iowa State University Press, Des Moines, 1990.
12 B. Bailyn, *New York Review of Books*, 20 Feb. 1998.
13 D. C. Watt, *Times Literary Supplement*, 10 April 1998.
14 Chalk & Jonassohn, op. cit.
15 J. Morris, 'The Final Solution down under', in Chalk & Jonassohn, ibid., pp. 205–22.
16 ibid.
17 ibid., pp. 206–8.
18 Colonial Secretary: In Letters, TSA, COL/1/323, p. 303.
19 Committee for the Aborigines Records, 17 Feb.–16 Sept. 1830, TSA, CBE/1, p. 7.
20 Colonial Secretary: In Letters, op. cit., p. 380.
21 ibid., p. 373.
22 1 Dec. 1826.
23 26 Feb. 1830.
24 10 Sept. 1831.
25 24 Sept. 1831.
26 *Hobart Town Courier*, 23 Jan. 1830.
27 24 Sept. 1830.
28 N. J. B. Plomley (ed.), *Friendly Mission*, THRA, Hobart, 1966, p. 435.

29 *Colonial Times*, 24 Sept. 1830.

30 ibid.

31 HRA 1, vol. XII, p. 125.

32 ibid., p. 21.

33 Huskisson to Arthur, 6 May 1828, Inward Dispatches, TSA 60/1/7, vol. 2, p. 109.

34 Murray to Arthur, 20 Feb. 1829, Inward Dispatches, TSA 60/1/9/1829, p. 141.

35 Murray to Arthur, 25 Aug. 1829, ibid., p. 233.

36 Murray to Arthur, 5 Nov. 1830, Inward Dispatches, TSA 60/1/11, vol. 16, p. 421.

37 ibid.

38 Goderich to Arthur, 17 June 1831, in Shaw, op. cit., p. 75.

39 Murray to Arthur, loc. cit.

40 Shaw, op. cit., p. 19.

41 ibid., pp. 21–2.

42 Arthur to Goderich, 10 Jan. 1828, in Shaw, op. cit., p. 3.

43 Arthur's Minute, 30 Nov. 1827, Colonial Secretary Files, TSA, CSO/1/170–4072, p. 21.

44 Memo to Captain Clark, ibid., p. 24.

45 Arthur to Huskisson, 17 April 1828, ibid., p. 5.

46 Governor's Office Papers, TSA, GO 33/7, p. 901.

47 See H. Reynolds, *Fate of a Free People*, Penguin, Ringwood, 1995, p. 110.

48 Arthur to Murray, 4 Nov. 1828, in Shaw, op. cit., p. 9.

49 Executive Council Minutes, 31 Oct. 1828, ibid., p. 11.

50 Shaw, op. cit., p. 12.

51 ibid.

Chapter 5:
Tasmania: The Black Line and
Wybalenna

1   Arthur to Murray, 20 Nov. 1830, in Shaw, op. cit., pp. 58–9.

2   Government Order, 9 Sept. 1830, ibid., p. 66.

3   Government Order, 22 Sept. 1830, ibid., p. 70.

4   Anstey to Cox, 13 Oct. 1830, Colonial Secretary Files, TSA, CSO/1/324.

5   Burnett to Lyttleton, 17 Sept. 1830, Colonial Secretary Files, TSA, CSO/1/317.

6   Colonial Secretary Files, TSA, CSO/1/329, p. 23.

7   Burnett to Arthur, 15 Oct. 1830, Letters from J. Burnett, 1826–34, TSA, FM4/3673, 15/2175.

8   ibid., 18 Oct. 1830.

9   ibid., 20 Oct. 1830.

10 ibid., 23 Oct. 1830.

11 ibid., 4 Nov. 1830.

12 ibid., 11 Nov. 1830.

13 Shaw, op. cit., p. 60.

14 J. Bonwick, *The Last of the Tasmanians*, Sampson Low, London, 1870, p. 226.

15 Plomley, op. cit., p. 350.

16 ibid., p. 196.

17 ibid., p. 197.

18 Executive Council Minutes, 27 Aug. 1830, TSA, EC, p. 566.

19 Arthur to Murray, 20 Nov. 1830, ibid., p. 58.

20 Executive Council Minutes, ibid., p. 64.

21 Aborigines Committee Minutes, 24 Oct. 1831, TSA, CBE/1, p. 135.

22 Colonial Secretary Files, TSA, CSO/1/317, p. 73.
23 Shaw, op. cit., p. 28.
24 A. Bell-Fialkoff, *Ethnic Cleansing*, St Martins, New York, 1996, p. 3.
25 Arthur to Murray, 20 Nov. 1830, in Shaw, op. cit., p. 60.
26 Aborigines Committee Minutes, 19 March 1830, ibid., p. 41.
27 ibid., p. 42.
28 Fein, op. cit., p. 21.
29 Hughes, op. cit., p. 423.
30 Diamond, op. cit., p. 10.
31 Morris, op. cit., pp. 217–18.
32 *Nulyarimma v. Thompson*, op. cit., p. 6.
33 Arthur to Goderich, 10 Jan. 1828, in Shaw, op. cit., p. 4.
34 ibid., p. 81.
35 ibid., p. 82.
36 ibid., p. 79.
37 Arthur to Darling, n.d., Colonial Secretary Files, TSA, COL/1/49/10853 (6), p. 105.
38 Darling to Arthur, 24 June 1834, in N. J. B. Plomley, *Weep in Silence*, Blubber Head Press, Hobart, 1987, pp. 1001–2.
39 Darling to Arthur, 20 Feb. 1833, ibid., p. 999.
40 Plomley, *Weep in Silence*, op. cit., p. 355.
41 Arthur's memo, 21 May 1835, TSA, CSO/1/803/17, p. 181.
42 Plomley, *Weep in Silence*, loc. cit.
43 ibid., p. 353.
44 Ryan to Robinson, 18 July 1836, ibid., p. 644.
45 Report of Major Ryan, G. A. Robinson Papers, ML, A7063, vol. 42.
46 Dr Jeanneret, 31 March 1847, TSA, CSO/11/26/455, p. 261.
47 Denison to Grey, 3 Dec. 1847, TSA, CSO/24/8/1318, p. 284.
48 J. Birmingham, 'Recent archaeology of Flinders Island', *Australian Natural History*, June 1973, p. 330.
49 J. West, *The History of Tasmania* [1852], ed. A. G. L. Shaw, Angus & Robertson, Sydney, 1971, p. 311.
50 Plomley, *Weep in Silence*, op. cit., pp. 356, 669.
51 ibid., p. 329.
52 Reynolds, *Fate of a Free People*, op. cit, pp. 7–8.

Chapter 6:
The impending catastrophe

1 Gipps to Glenelg, 6 April 1839, HRA 1, vol. XX, p. 91.
2 J. Stephen, memo on Gipps to Glenelg, 6 April 1839, CO/201/285.
3 ibid.
4 Gipps to Glenelg, 21 July 1838, HRA 1, vol. XIX, pp. 509–10.
5 J. Stephen, memo on Gipps to Glenelg, 22 July 1839, CO/201/286.
6 J. Stephen, memo on Gipps to Russell, 9 April 1841, CO/201/309.
7 J. Stephen, memo on Gipps to Russell, 19 July 1841, CO/201/310.
8 J. Stephen, memo on Gipps to Russell, 26 Sept. 1841, CO/201/311.
9 J. Stephen, memo on Gipps to Stanley, 4 Jan. 1843, CO/201/331.
10 J. Stephen, memo on Gipps to Russell, 9 April 1841, CO/201/309.

11   UN, Ad Hoc Committee, 7 April
     1948, E/AC.25/12.
12   J. Backhouse, *A Narrative of a Visit to
     the Australian Colonies*, Hamilton,
     Adams, London, 1843, p. 558.
13   J. L. Stokes, *Discoveries in Australia*,
     T. & W. Boone, London, 1846,
     vol. II, p. 459.
14   W. Thomas, 21 June 1839,
     Correspondence & Returns,
     1838–45, ML, uncat. ms.
15   W. Thomas to G. A. Robinson,
     6 Aug. 1839, ibid.
16   Answer to circular from NSW
     Legislative Council, 1845, p. 93,
     G. A. Robinson Papers, ML,
     mss A7078/1.
17   G. A. Robinson, Journal, 18 Jan.–
     2 Feb. 1840, ML, mss A7036/1.
18   G. A. Robinson, Annual Report,
     1846; Letterbook 1845–48, ML,
     mss A7081.
19   G. A. Robinson, Journal, 25 April–
     6 July 1839, ML, mss A7035.
20   Letter, Encounter Bay, 8 Dec. 1840,
     Anti-Slavery Society Papers, Rhodes
     House, Oxford, S.18/C159.
21   J. Warman, in *Port Phillip Herald*,
     21 Jan. 1847.
22   *Perth Gazette*, 22 July 1837.
23   G. C. Mundy, *Our Antipodes*,
     Richard Bentley, London, 1857,
     pp. 230–5.
24   E. Eyre, *Journals of Expeditions of
     Discovery*, T. & W. Boone, London,
     1845, vol. 1, p. 170.
25   XZX, pseud., 'The Aborigines
     protectors', *Colonist*, 21 Nov. 1838.
26   T. Bartlett, *New Holland*, Longman,
     London, 1843, pp. 65–6.
27   NSW, Legislative Council 1839, *Votes

     & Proceedings*, Commission on Police
     & Gaols, pp. 224–5.
28   HRA 1, vol. XXV.
29   4 May 1839.
30   Letter 'Black versus white',
     Stat Umbra, *Colonist*, 16 Feb. 1839.
31   F. Eldershaw, *Australia as It Really Is*,
     Darton & Co., London, 1854,
     pp. 63–73.

Chapter 7:
Dispersing the blacks

1   Memo by Earl Grey on dispatch,
     Fitzroy to Grey, 17 May 1847,
     CO/201/382.
2   Grey to Fitzroy, 10 Feb. 1850,
     CO/208/58.
3   K. Waler, The Letters of the Leslie
     Brothers from Australia, B.A. Hons
     thesis, University of Queensland,
     1956, p. 85.
4   M. French, *Conflict on the Condamine*,
     Darling Downs Institute Press,
     Toowoomba, 1989, p. 95.
5   C. P. Hodgson, *Reminiscences of
     Australia*, W. N. Wright, London,
     1846, p. 223.
6   NSW, Legislative Council 1858, *Votes
     & Proceedings*, Select Committee on
     the Aborigines Question, p. 7.
7   Queensland, 1861, *Votes &
     Proceedings*, Select Committee on the
     Native Police Force, pp. 151–2.
8   ibid., p. 17.
9   *Queensland Guardian*, 27 July 1861.
10   ibid., 4 May 1861.
11   *Moreton Bay Courier*, 27 July 1861.
12   ibid., 26 July 1861.
13   Mr Moffatt, *Queensland Guardian*,
     4 May 1861.
14   ibid., 27 July 1861.

15   ibid.

16   'Australian', 'The murder of Mr Wills', *Queensland Guardian*, 6 Nov. 1861.

17   *The Way We Civilise* (series of articles reprinted from the *Queenslander*), G. & J. Black, Brisbane, 1880, p. 4.

18   ibid.

19   Queensland, 1880, *Parliamentary Debates*, vol. XXXIII, p. 1134.

20   ibid., p. 1137.

21   ibid.

22   ibid.

23   Palmer to Howitt, 5 Aug. 1882, Howitt Papers, Box 5, Folder 1, National Museum of Victoria.

24   Queensland, 1880, op. cit., vol. XXXIII, p. 665.

25   ibid., p. 676.

26   ibid., p. 666.

27   *Brisbane Courier*, 2 April 1861.

28   Truth, 'Legalized murder of Aborigines', *Brisbane Courier*, 6 April 1861.

29   6 April 1876.

30   10 Jan. 1877.

31   20 Nov. 1869.

32   Glenelg to Bourke, 26 July 1837, HRA 1, vol. XIX, p. 48.

33   *Brisbane Courier*, 26 July 1861.

34   Queensland, 1880, op. cit., vol. XXXIII, p. 673.

35   Quoted by T. Douglas in Queensland, 1880, op. cit., vol. XXXIII, p. 1134.

36   6 April 1876.

37   North Gregory, in *Queenslander*, 12 June 1880.

38   Queensland, 1880, op. cit., vol. XXXIII, p. 1141.

39   15 Feb. 1879.

40   8 Nov. 1870.

41   23 March 1858.

42   *Moreton Bay Courier*, 7 May 1859.

43   *Queenslander*, 8 March 1879.

44   26 Nov. 1887.

45   C. Lumholtz, *Among Cannibals*, Charles Scribner's Sons, London, 1889, p. 153.

46   *Queenslander*, 28 Feb. 1874.

47   'Never-Never', *Queenslander*, 8 May 1880.

48   21 Feb. 1878.

49   Queensland, 1876, *Parliamentary Debates*, vol. XXIX, p. 1423.

50   6 Dec. 1861.

51   *North Australian*, 27 July 1861.

52   4 May 1861.

53   8 May 1858.

54   Reprinted in *Queenslander*, 31 March 1866.

55   'Never-Never', op. cit.

56   North Gregory, op. cit.

57   2 Feb. 1859.

58   6 Aug. 1867.

59   4 May 1861.

Chapter 8:
Sudden and terrible retribution

1   Reported in *Sydney Morning Herald*, 16 June 1858.

2   17 Nov. 1857.

3   11 May 1858.

4   19 May 1858.

5   17 Nov. 1857.

6   *North Australian*, 3 Aug. 1858.

7   *Moreton Bay Courier*, 23 April 1859.

8   F. Sinnett, *Account of the 'Rush' to Port Curtis*, Geelong, 1859, p. 71.

9   'Australian', op. cit.

10   ibid.

11   *Queensland Guardian*, 9 Nov. 1861.

12   ibid., 11 Dec. 1861.

13   ibid., 21 Dec. 1861.

14   Quoted by R. Evans in R. Evans,
K. Saunders & K. Cronin, *Race
Relations in Colonial Queensland*,
University of Queensland Press,
St Lucia, 1988, p. 52.

15   6 Nov. 1861.

16   G. Reid, *A Nest of Hornets*, Oxford
University Press, Melbourne, 1982,
p. ix.

17   As quoted by Reid, ibid., p. 89.

18   Quoted by Evans in *Race Relations*,
op. cit., p. 375.

19   Reid, op. cit., p. 96.

20   W. Telfer, Reminiscences, ML mss
A2376, p. 88.

21   Reid, op. cit., p. 178.

22   *Queensland Times*, 13 Dec. 1861.

23   Reid, op. cit., p. 134.

24   11 Dec. 1861.

25   12 Dec. 1861.

26   His two-volume *History of Tasmania*
of 1852 is the most distinguished
history written in colonial Australia.

27   Quoted by Reid, loc. cit.

28   J. B. Jukes, *Narrative of Surveying
Voyage of H.M.S. Fly*, T. & W. Boone,
London, 1847, p. 114.

29   P. L. Watson, *Frontier Lands and
Pioneer Legends*, Allen & Unwin,
St Leonards, 1998.

30   M. Durack, *Kings in Grass Castles*,
Constable, London, 1959, p. 137.

31   ibid., p. 138.

32   L. Hercus, 'Glimpses of the
Karanguru', *Records of South
Australian Museum*, vol. 25, no. 2,
p. 156.

33   ibid, p. 157.

34   ibid, p. 158.

35   Watson, op. cit., p. 3.

36   P. L. Watson, 'Passed away? The fate
of the Karuwali', unpublished paper,
p. 21.

37   ibid., p. 36.

38   R. Kimber, *Genocide or Not?
The Situation in Central Australia,
1860–1895*, Centre for Comparative
Genocide Studies, Macquarie
University, Sydney, 1997.

39   ibid., p. 60. See also D. J. Mulvaney,
Encounters in Place, University of
Queensland Press, St Lucia, 1989,
pp. 123–30; M. Hartwig, The
Progress of White Settlement in
the Alice Springs District . . .
1860–1914, Ph.D. thesis, University
of Adelaide, 1965.

40   Western Australia, 1893, *Debates*,
p. 1050.

41   R. McGregor, 'Law enforcement or
just force? Police action in two
frontier districts', in H. Reynolds
(ed.), *Race Relations in North
Queensland*, James Cook University,
Townsville, 1993, p. 80.

42   A. Gill, 'Aborigines, settlers and
police in the Kimberleys 1887–1905',
Studies in Western Australian History,
vol. 1, June 1977, p. 18.

43   McGregor, loc. cit.

44   Noonkanbah Station with a
population of over 200. H. Pedersen
& B. Woorunmurra, *Tandamarra*,
Magabala Books, Broome, 1995,
p. 136.

45   Quoted by Gill, op. cit., p. 17.

Chapter 9:
A dying race

1   Quoted by R. McGregor in *Imagined
Destinies: Aboriginal Australians and the*

Doomed Race Theory, 1880–1939, Melbourne University Press, Carlton, 1997, p. 13.

2   Scott to Darling, 1 Aug. 1827, Scott Letterbooks, ML mss A850.

3   ibid.

4   Letter from a Gentleman in New South Wales, Oct. 1826, Methodist Missionary Society, In Correspondence: Australia, 1812–26, Folder 4, Australian Joint Copying Project.

5   ibid.

6   ibid.

7   Stirling to Aberdeen, 10 July 1835, Dispatches to the Colonial Office, 14 Sept. 1834– 6 Dec. 1838, Battye Library.

8   24 Oct. 1838, as quoted in J. N. Molony, *An Architect of Freedom*, ANU Press, Canberra, 1973, p. 138.

9   26 Dec. 1836, as quoted in Molony, op. cit., p. 136.

10   29 Jan. 1852.

11   'The Aborigines' by T__, 30 Nov. 1858.

12   T. McCombie, *The History of the Colony of Victoria*, Sands & Kenny, Melbourne, 1858, p. 88.

13   P. de Strzelecki, *Physical Description of New South Wales and Van Diemen's Land*, Longman, London, 1845, p. 344.

14   ibid.

15   J. D. Lang, *An Historical and Statistical Account of New South Wales*, 4th edn, Sampson Low, London, 1875, vol. 1, p. 28.

16   C. Darwin, *Journal of Researches . . . etc.*, Henry Colburn, London, 1839, p. 520.

17   H. Merivale, *Lectures on Colonization and Colonies*, 2nd edn, Oxford University Press, London, 1928, p. 540.

18   Lang, loc. cit.

19   J. Bonwick, *Port Phillip Settlement*, Sampson Low, London, 1883, p. iv.

20   *Brisbane Courier*, 25 March 1865.

21   Stokes, op. cit., pp. 463–4.

22   *Rockhampton Bulletin*, 6 Aug. 1867.

23   West, op. cit., p. 94.

24   25 March 1865.

25   13 Jan. 1881.

26   A.C.G., 5 June 1880.

27   A. L. Cameron, *Journal of the Anthropological Institute*, vol. XIV, 1885, p. 344.

28   Queensland, 1889, *Votes & Proceedings*, 5, Report of the Scientific Expedition to Bellendern Ker Range, p. 1213.

29   A.C.G., op. cit.

30   A. G. Sutherland, *Victoria and Its Metropolis*, McCarron, Bird, Melbourne, 1888, vol. 1, p. 29.

31   J. Collier, *The Pastoral Age in Australasia*, Whitcombe & Tombs, London, 1911, p. 135.

32   13 Jan. 1881.

33   *Queenslander*, 8 May 1880.

34   6 Aug. 1867.

35   Cited by R. McGregor, op. cit., p. 55.

36   Cited by P. Jacobs in 'Science and veiled assumptions, etc.', *Australian Aboriginal Studies*, vol. 2, 1986, p. 16.

37   W. B. Spencer & F. J. Gillen, *The Native Tribes of Central Australia*, Macmillan, London, 1899, p. xiii.

38   Report of the 15th Meeting of the Australian Association for the Advancement of Science, 1921, p. lxxxix.

39   W. L. Cleland, in *Proceedings of Royal Society of South Australia*, vol. 23, 1898–99, p. 302.

40   Cited by R. McGregor, op. cit., p. 57.

41   J. B. Cleland, 'Disease among the Australian Aborigines', *Journal of Tropical Medicine and Hygiene*, vol. 31, Feb. 1928, p. 53.

42   J. W. Bleakley, 'Can our Aborigines be preserved?', *Australian Quarterly*, vol. 7, Sept. 1930, p. 61.

43   Queensland, 1933, *Votes & Proceedings*, p. 889.

44   Australia, Parliament 1914–15, *Report of Administrator of the Northern Territory for 1914–15*, Parliamentary Paper 240, Canberra, p. 27.

45   Cook to Administrator, 29 June 1933, Dept of Interior, Australian Archives CRS A659, 40/1/408.

46   Cook to Morley, 29 April 1931, cited in McGregor, op. cit., p. 170.

47   Cook to Administrator, 27 June 1933, Dept of Interior, Australian Archives CRS A659, 40/1/408.

48   Cook to Administrator, 7 Feb. 1933, cited in McGregor, op. cit., p. 161.

49   ibid., p. 162.

50   T. Austin, *Never Trust a Government Man: Northern Territory Aboriginal Policy 1911–1939*, NTU Press, Darwin, 1997, p. 197.

51   McGregor, op. cit., p. 173.

52   Cited in P. Jacobs, *Mister Neville*, Fremantle Arts Centre Press, Fremantle, 1990, p. 18.

53   ibid., p. 16.

54   ibid., p. 221.

55   ibid., p. 193.

56   Conference Report, Dept of Native Affairs, ACC.993, 427/36, Dept of Native Affairs Archive, Perth.

57   ibid.

58   *Aboriginal Welfare: Initial Conference of Commonwealth and State Aboriginal Authorities*, Commonwealth Govt Printer, Canberra, 1937, p. 5.

Chapter 10:
'The same manner of living'

1   W. M. Horton to Wesleyan Mission Society, 2 June 1823, Bonwick Transcripts, Box 52, ML.

2   Letter from a Gentleman, op. cit.

3   *Colonist*, 24 Oct. 1838.

4   ibid.

5   Bonwick Transcripts, Box 50, p. 476, ML.

6   CMS to Porter, 2 Feb. 1838: Missionaries, NSW Archives, 4/2409.2.

7   Queensland, 1908, *Votes & Proceedings*, Annual Report of the Chief Protector of Aborigines for 1907, vol. III, p. 944.

8   HRA 1, vol. XXII, p. 125.

9   *Report from the Select Committee on Aborigines (British Settlements)*, British Parliamentary Papers, 1837, 7, 425, pp. 4–5.

10   Macquarie to Bathurst, 8 Oct. 1814, HRA 1, vol. VIII, p. 369.

11   Cited by P. B. Walsh in The Problems of Native Policy in South Australia in the Nineteenth Century, BA Hons thesis, University of Adelaide, 1966, p. 19.

12   Scott to Sadlier, 29 July 1826, T. H. Scott Letterbook, ML A850.

13   11 Aug. 1810.

14   NSW, Legislative Council 1846, *Votes*

& *Proceedings*, Replies to Circular Letters addressed to the Clergy, p. 563.

15 NSW, Legislative Council 1849, *Votes & Proceedings*, Select Committee on the Aborigines and the Protectorate, p. 37.

16 C. Sturt, *Narrative of an Expedition into Central Australia*, T. & W. Boone, London, 1849, vol. 2, pp. 284–5.

17 ibid.

18 Harper to Newstead, 23 April 1827, Bonwick Transcripts, Box 53, ML.

19 M. B. Hale, *The Aborigines of Australia*, Society for Promoting Christian Knowledge, London, c. 1889, p. 66.

20 ibid., p. 53.

21 Chatfield to Attorney-General, n.d., Colonial Secretary, In Letters, Queensland State Archives, COL/A1483 of 1869.

22 Henry to Colonial Secretary, 29 Sept. 1874, ibid., COL/A2913.

23 H. Wade-Broun, *Memoirs of a Queensland Pioneer*, Sandgate, 1944, p. 18.

24 Western Australia, 1886, *Parliamentary Papers*, Select Committee on the Aborigines Protection Bill, A6.

25 Queensland, 1903, *Votes & Proceedings*, vol. 2, p. 461.

26 Ordinance no. 16 of 1911, cited by R. MacDonald in *Between Two Worlds*, IAD Press, Alice Springs, 1966, p. 13.

27 A. Haebich, *For Their Own Good*, University of Western Australia Press, Nedlands, 1988, p. 156.

28 *Bringing Them Home*, op. cit., p. 275.

29 ibid., pp. 272–3.

30 ibid., p. 273.

31 ibid., p. 274.

32 ibid.

33 Cited by S. Stone (ed.), in *Aborigines in White Australia*, Heinemann, South Yarra, 1974, p. 192.

34 P. Hasluck, *Shades of Darkness*, Melbourne University Press, Carlton, 1988, p. 93.

35 The articles were republished in a pamphlet: *Our Southern Half-caste Natives and Their Conditions*, Native Welfare Council, Perth, 1938, p. 1.

36 ibid.

37 ibid., p. 4.

38 ibid., p. 3.

39 ibid., p. 2.

40 ibid., p. 22.

41 ibid., p. 23.

42 ibid., p. 27.

43 ibid., p. 24.

44 Australia, House of Representatives, 1950, *Debates*, vol. 208, p. 3977.

45 Address to Section F, 29th ANZAAS Congress, Sydney, Aug. 1952, Hasluck Papers, Australian National Library, 5274, Box 38.

46 P. Hasluck, 'The problem of assimilation', in R. M. & C. H. Berndt (eds), *Aboriginal Man in Australia*, Angus & Robertson, Sydney, 1968, p. 435.

47 Cited by T. Rowse in 'The modesty of the State', in T. Stannage et al. (eds), *Paul Hasluck in Australian History*, University of Queensland Press, St Lucia, n.d., p. 124.

48 ibid.

49 Native Welfare: An Address to National Council of Women,

Melbourne, Oct. 1952, p. 8.
Hasluck Papers, op. cit.

50 Australia, House of Representatives
    1951, *Parliamentary Debates*, vol. 214,
    p. 874.
51 ibid.
52 ibid., p. 875.
53 New Hope for Old Australians,
    Wesley Church, Melbourne, 14 July
    1957, Hasluck Papers, op. cit.
54 ibid.
55 Speech on the Estimates, 6 Oct.
    1955, Hasluck Papers, op. cit.
56 ibid.
57 Australia, House of Representatives
    1951, op. cit., p. 876.

Conclusion
1 UN General Assembly, Third
   Session, Official Records, Part 1,
   83rd meeting of Sixth Committee,
   1948 (25 Oct.), p. 186.
2 ibid., p. 195.
3 UN, *Draft Convention*, op. cit., p. 27.
4 UN, Ad Hoc Committee on

Genocide, 14th meeting, 21 April
1948, E/AC.25/SR.14.

5 UN, 63rd meeting of Sixth
   Committee, 1948 (30 Sept.), p. 4.
6 UN, 65th meeting of Sixth
   Committee, 1948 (2 Oct.),
   p. 24.
7 UN, 83rd meeting of Sixth
   Committee, op. cit., p. 199.
8 UN General Assembly, Third
   Session, Official Records, Part 1,
   Economic and Social Council, 7th
   Session, 1948, p. 719.
9 UN, 63rd meeting of Sixth
   Committee, op. cit., p. 7.
10 UN, 83rd meeting of Sixth
   Committee, op. cit., p. 198.
11 ibid.
12 See P. Thornberry, *Minorities and
   Human Rights Law*, Minorities Rights
   Group, London, 1991, p. 14.
13 UN Human Rights Committee,
   General Comment no. 23 (50),
   1994, CA Supplement (A49/40),
   pp. 108–9.

FURTHER READING

There is an extensive international literature on the question of genocide and related topics. The best place to begin is with Raphael Lemkin's *Axis Rule in Occupied Europe* (Carnegie Endowment for International Peace, Washington, 1944). Among the most useful of the many books published in the last twenty years are:

Andreopoulos, G. J. (ed.), *Genocide: Conceptual and Historical Dimensions*, University of Pennsylvania Press, Philadelphia, 1994.

Bell-Fialkoff, A., *Ethnic Cleansing*, St Martins, New York, 1996.

Chalk, F. & Jonassohn, K., *The History and Sociology of Genocide*, Yale University Press, New Haven, 1990.

Churchill, W., *A Little Matter of Genocide: Holocaust and Denial in the Americas, 1492 to the Present*, City Lights Books, San Francisco, 1997.

Dobkowski M. & Wallimann, I. (eds), *Genocide and the Modern Age*, Greenwood, New York, 1987.

Fein, H., *Genocide: A Sociological Perspective*, Sage, London, 1990.

Fein, H. (ed.), *Genocide Watch*, Yale University Press, New Haven, 1992.

Jonassohn, K. & Bjornson, K. S., *Genocide and Gross Human Rights Violations in Comparative Perspective*, Transaction Publishers, London, 1998.

Katz, S. T., *The Holocaust in Historical Context*, vol. 1, Oxford University Press, New York, 1994.

Kuper, L., *Genocide*, Penguin, Harmondsworth, 1981.

Mazian, F., *Why Genocide?*, Iowa State University Press, Des Moines, 1990.

Strozier, C. B. & Flynn, M. (eds), *Genocide, War and Human Survival*, Rowman & Littlefield, Lanham, Maryland, 1996.

The literature of genocide in Australia is much more limited, but includes the following:

Barta, T., 'After the Holocaust: consciousness of genocide in Australia', *Australian Journal of Politics and History*, vol. 31, no. 1, 1984, pp. 154–61.

— 'Relations of genocide: land and lives in the colonization of Australia', in M. Dobkowski & I. Wallimann, eds. *Genocide and the Modern Age*, Greenwood, New York, 1987, pp. 237–51.

Moses, A. D., 'An antipodean genocide? The origins of the genocidal moment in the colonization of Australia', *Journal of Genocide Research*, vol. 2, no. 1, 2000, pp. 89–106.

Palmer, A., *Colonial Genocide*, Crawford House, Bathurst, 2000.

Tatz, C., *Genocide in Australia*, Aboriginal Studies Press, Canberra, 1999.

For the controversy surrounding genocide and the stolen generation, refer to *Bringing Them Home: National Inquiry into the Separation of Aboriginal and Torres Strait Islander Children from Their Families*, Human Rights & Equal Opportunity Commission, Sydney, 1997. Among the extensive commentary on the question are the following:

Brenton, R., 'Genocide and the "stolen generation"', *Quadrant*, vol. XLII, no. 5, May 1998, pp. 19–24.

Gaita, R., 'Genocide and pedantry', *Quadrant*, vol. XLI, nos 7 & 8, July/Aug. 1997, pp. 41–5.

Haebich, A., *Broken Circles: Fragmenting Indigenous Families 1800–2000*,

Fremantle Arts Centre Press, Fremantle, 2000.

Manne, R., 'In denial: the stolen generation and the Right', *Australian Quarterly Essay*, no. 1, 2001.

Markus, A., *Race: John Howard and the Remaking of Australia*, Allen & Unwin, Crows Nest, NSW, 2001.

Minogue, K. 'Aborigines and Australian apologetics', *Quadrant*, vol. XLII, no. 9, Sept. 1998, pp. 11–20.

The controversy about the smallpox epidemic can be followed in:

Butlin, N. G., *Close Encounters of the Worst Kind: Modelling Aboriginal Depopulation and Resource Competition 1788–1850*, Working Paper in Economic History no. 8, ANU, Canberra, 1982.

— *Economics and the Dreamtime*, Cambridge University Press, Melbourne, 1993.

— *Macassans and Aboriginal Smallpox: The 1789 and 1829 Epidemics*, Working Paper in Economic History no. 22, ANU, Canberra, 1984.

— *Our Original Aggression: Aboriginal Populations of Southeastern Australia 1788–1850*, Allen & Unwin, Sydney, 1983.

Campbell, J., 'Smallpox in Aboriginal Australia: the early 1830s', *Historical Studies*, vol. 21, no. 84, April 1985, pp. 336–58.

— 'Whence came the pox?', *Age Monthly Review*, vol. 3, no. 10, Feb. 1984, pp. 19–20.

Day, D., *Claiming a Continent: A History of Australia*, Angus & Robertson, Pymble, 1996.

Frost, A., *Botany Bay Mirages: Illusions of Australia's Convict Beginnings*, Melbourne University Press, Carlton, 1994.

Wilson, C., 'History, hypothesis and fiction', *Quadrant*, vol. XXIX, no. 3, March 1985, pp. 26–32.

Many of the books on genocide contain passing remarks about Tasmania, but for more detailed material, see:

Plomley, N. J. B., *The Aboriginal/Settler Clash in Van Diemen's Land, 1803–1831*, Queen Victoria Museum & Art Gallery, Launceston,

1992.

Pybus, C., *Community of Thieves*, Heinemann, Port Melbourne, 1991.

Reynolds, H., *Fate of a Free People*, Penguin, Ringwood, 1995.

Ryan, L. *The Aboriginal Tasmanians*, University of Queensland Press, St Lucia, 1981.

There are many books on the subject of nineteenth-century frontier conflict, but the following are particularly relevant:

Clark, I., *Scars in the Landscape: A Register of Massacre Sites in Western Victoria 1803–1859*, Aboriginal Studies Press, Canberra, 1995.

Critchett, J., *A Distant Field of Murder: Western District Frontiers, 1834–1848*, Melbourne University Press, Carlton, 1992.

Evans, R., Saunders, K., & Cronin, K., *Race Relations in Colonial Queensland*, University of Queensland Press, St Lucia, 1988.

French, M., *Conflict on the Condamine*, Darling Downs Institute Press, Toowoomba, 1989.

Goodall, H., *Invasion to Embassy: Land in Aboriginal Politics in New South Wales, 1770–1972*, Allen & Unwin, St Leonards, 1996.

Loos, N. *Invasion and Resistance: Aboriginal–European Relations on the North Queensland Frontier 1861–1897*, ANU Press, Canberra, 1982.

Read, P., *A Hundred Years War: The Wiradjuri People and the State*, ANU Press, Canberra, 1988.

Reynolds, H., *The Other Side of the Frontier: Aboriginal Resistance to the European Invasion of Australia*, Penguin, Ringwood, 1982.

—— *Frontier: Aborigines, Settlers and Land*, Allen & Unwin, Sydney, 1987.

Rowley, C. D., *The Destruction of Aboriginal Society*, ANU Press, Canberra, 1970.

Watson, P. L., *Frontier Lands and Pioneer Legends*, Allen & Unwin, St Leonards, 1998.

For material on the concept of the dying race, refer to McGregor, R., *Imagined Destinies: Aboriginal Australians and the Doomed Race Theory, 1880–1939*, Melbourne University Press, Carlton, 1997.

For the policies of the 1920s and 1930s, consult:

Austin, T., *Never Trust a Government Man: Northern Territory Aboriginal Policy 1911–1939*, NTU Press, Darwin, 1997.

Beresford, Q. & Omaji, P., *Our State of Mind: Racial Planning and the Stolen Generations*, Fremantle Arts Centre Press, Fremantle, 1998.

Haebich, A., *For Their Own Good: Aborigines and Government in the Southwest of Western Australia, 1900–1940*, University of Western Australia Press, Nedlands, 1988.

Jacobs, P., *Mister Neville*, Fremantle Arts Centre Press, Fremantle, 1990.

Kidd, R., *The Way We Civilise: Aboriginal Affairs – The Untold Story*, University of Queensland Press, St Lucia, 1997.

For a discussion of the ideas and policies of Sir Paul Hasluck, see:

Hasluck, P., *Shades of Darkness: Aboriginal Affairs, 1925–1965*, Melbourne University Press, Carlton, 1988.

— *Mucking About: An Autobiography*, Melbourne University Press, Carlton, 1977.

Stannage, T., et al. (eds), *Paul Hasluck in Australian History*, University of Queensland Press, St Lucia, n.d.

INDEX

WHY WEREN'T WE TOLD?

Henry Reynolds

Why were we never told? Why didn't we know?

Historian Henry Reynolds has found himself being asked these questions by many people, over many years, in all parts of Australia. The acclaimed *Why Weren't We Told?* is a frank account of his personal journey towards the realisation that he, like generations of Australians, grew up with a distorted and idealised version of the past. From the author's unforgettable encounter in a North Queensland jail with injustice towards Aboriginal children, to his friendship with Eddie Mabo, to his shattering of the myths about our 'peaceful' history, this bestselling book will shock, move and intrigue. *Why Weren't We Told?* is crucial reading on the most important debate in Australia as we enter the twenty-first century.

'This is a fine and engaging memoir. It is also a fascinating book about the writing of history, by one of its master practitioners in this country.'
Michael Duffy, *The Australian*

'*Why Weren't We Told?* urges us to continue to search for the truth about our past in order to prepare for and safeguard our future.'
Andrea Durbach, *The Bulletin*

'A must-read . . . I found the story of Reynolds's intellectual and spiritual journey moving and thought-provoking.'
Noel Pearson, *The Age*

Winner of the 1999 Australian Human Rights Award for the Arts

BLACK PIONEERS

Henry Reynolds

Black Pioneers is an important new edition of *With the White People*, Henry Reynolds's challenging account of the role of Aboriginal and Islander people in the exploration and development of colonial Australia.

In this book, Henry Reynolds debunks the notion that indigenous peoples have contributed nothing towards the creation of a prosperous modern society, that modern Australia rests on the sturdy foundations put down in the nineteenth century by the European pioneers.

Black Pioneers pays tribute to the labour and skill of the thousands of black men, women and children who worked for the Europeans in a wide range of occupations: as interpreters, concubines, trackers, troopers, servants, nursemaids, labourers, stockworkers and pearl-divers. Some of their intriguing stories are here revealed.

Featuring a timely new introductory essay, *Black Pioneers* is an essential contribution to Australian history at a time when examining our shared past has never been more crucial.

THE LAW OF THE LAND

Henry Reynolds

'I am at a loss to conceive by what tenure we hold this country, for it does not appear to be that we either hold it by conquest or by right of purchase.'

G. A. Robinson, 1832

In this readable and dramatic book, Henry Reynolds reassesses the legal and political arguments used to justify the European settlement of Australia. His conclusions form a compelling case for the belief that the British government conceded land rights to the Aborigines early in the nineteenth century.